The Modern Artist's Way

How to Build a Successful Career as a Creative in the 21st Century

D1496520

The Modern Artist's Way

How to Build a Successful Career as a Creative in the 21st Century

BRIDGETTE MAYER

Printed by Ingramsparks

Cover Design: Pete Garceau

Typesetting: 2QT Publishing

ISBN - 978-0-578-60692-7

Dedication

To my partner in life, Tariq Johnson, who pushes me to be my best every day. I love you! To my little boy, Caleb Johnson. You are my reason why every morning when I wake up and see your joyful smiling face. I promise you that for anything you want to be in this life, I will light the way for you and be the best role model and Mom I can be for you. I love you!

Contents

Foreword: Getting Seen, Read and Heard

WHEN I WAS about four years old, my life was pretty bleak. I was living with my single, abusive mom in an apartment with no furniture or the typical toys a kid might have. One day, I found a ratty bag with makeup in it. As I played with the materials in the bag, I went over to one of the apartment walls and smeared the makeup everywhere, thus making my first piece of art. I remember it being fun, expressive and liberating. Something clicked for me in that moment.

Later, after I was adopted, I would go on making and creating things: mud drawings, paintings, collections of dried flowers that I'd catalog and put in books, and all kinds of buttons that I had in an old tin can which I loved to play with and organize. In High School, I learned more about the technical aspects of making art and explored working in ceramics and clay. My passion continued into college where I decided to major in Studio Art and Art History and to concentrate in the arts: painting, printmaking, sculpture, photography, art history and modern and contemporary art. I loved learning and making. The possibilities were endless.

The practical considerations of being in the industry always shadowed me. The more I learned about artists, the more I understood the 'starving artist' mentality that is a reality for most artists and is often part of being in the arts. I heard from many well-intentioned people in my life that I should consider doing something else more lucrative, because it is difficult to make it and thrive in the Art Business.

I knew that I would need to work hard; this was something that came easy to me when I started my first businesses at ages thirteen and sixteen. I was babysitting for $15.00 an hour and then cleaning houses for $18.00 an hour. My early work experiences made me certain that I would make money, that I would not starve and return to the horrific childhood conditions in which I lived before I was adopted. You can read my story about this, and about how I got my start in the Arts, in my book *The Art Cure: A Memoir of Abuse and Fortune* (Lioncrest Publishing 2016). Making money early on drew my attention and efforts toward creating more possibilities in my life. The question at that time was: how could I lay the foundation for this and for being in the industry that I loved: The Art World.

Whether you are an artist, a musician, a dancer, a writer, a gallerist, designer or any type of maker, producer or creative, the challenge is how to make a living and thrive doing what you are passionate about. Have you ever asked yourself any of these questions:

How do you get people to pay you for what you love doing?

How do you get your name known to the public?

How do you create your vision and have it come to life, while also dealing with possible rejection or cash flow issues?

And what about this Big Question:

How do you get on that higher path which will bring you a fulfilled life, one in which you will leave your legacy—whether it is to your family, your community or the world—and also make an impact?

By exploring these questions, you will discover, what I name, The Modern Artist's Way.

I will share a practical and thoughtful way to build foundations and to begin to create or to expand your art career or take an existing career to the next level.

Although I come from a Fine Arts background, this book is for any artist irrespective of what medium they are working in. In fact, you will learn in the middle of this book that sometimes the smartest thing you can do is crossover from one art form to another, or merge two or more forms together. This book is for anyone from high school age through retirement who wants to create a thriving career and obtain a bundle of ideas about how to do it. You will learn how to plan for and enjoy a profitable career. You will discover how to be successful while you are alive, and not posthumously, by creating a career you can enjoy and share in your lifetime.

We are living in a time when the entire paradigm of being a creative has shifted. We have access to more information and people than we have ever had at any point in time, and certainly more than when I started my gallery in 2001 (when many creatives were only just starting to have websites). Now with social media and other forms of global marketing and communication, we have exponentially more reach and access to channels that will help us grow, produce, create and thrive. It is my goal in this book to provide tools and ideas to help you tap into and harness this power to create and build your vision.

1. What Makes You Happy?

WHAT MAKES MOST artists happy is the creation process itself. They are in the flow when they go into their studios, offices and workshops to make their art and become fully absorbed in the process. They feel they are at their happiest when they do not have to worry about marketing, networking or selling or about whether a check will arrive every month. It is bliss not having to doing anything except what they love the most.

Most creatives would be very happy if someone said to them: "Just go off and create art all day, and I will pay you and send you a check at the end of each month."

I recently asked an artist what made her happy, and she told me that, besides getting to make a living as an artist and do it full time, there is a deeper level to her creation. Her real motivator is knowing that someone values what she has created enough to purchase it and bring it into their home or their world.

On the gallerist side, it is deeply gratifying for me to help a client to be able to identify a work of art for their space, want to invest money in purchasing it and have it bring joy to their life. I have seen the acquisition of art transform people's lives over many years by adding culture, color and relationships to their world. One of the things that makes me happiest about my work is helping someone add value to their life and home through their art collecting.

There are many recently published books and articles on happiness and I know, from observation, that most creatives want to feel a sense of accomplishment, success, and growth in their artwork and in the industry. Many at the highest levels want to make an important cultural impact and be famous. For some, overcoming challenges in their art will bring them this sense of accomplishment. There is a process to this.

In 2001, when I started my gallery at 26 years old, I wanted to work with younger artists coming out of graduate school who were in a similar place professionally. Although at this point I had worked in the art world in New York, San Francisco and overseas, my name was still pretty much unknown. It was the same for these younger artists, many of whom went from a four-year college studying art, like I had, into a two or three-year Master of Fine Arts graduate program. My thought was to forge partnerships with the artists I selected; we would build our careers together independent of graduate school and, for myself, independent of working for someone else.

I was incredibly happy and excited in this process of putting my program together, interviewing artists, visiting studios, and creating my vision each day. I had a very strong purpose and drive which was to create a top-notch gallery program, to not fail in the process and to be successful financially.

I faced many challenges in my first year. I opened in May of

2001 and, shortly thereafter, many people started their summer vacations, leaving the city from Thursday through Monday morning. At the time, I had no client list and many of my initial sales came from family or friends and family of the artists I was working with. These artists were happy to be involved with what was, for most of them, their first commercial gallery. At the time, I had a smallish space of 600 square feet, which also was a challenge for some of the artists who wanted to paint larger work, because they had to downsize what they were making to fit the space.

My next challenge came that September when the events of 9/11 happened. The whole world shut down afterwards in shock and fear for many months, as people suffered from loss and tried to recover. On that day, I sold the last piece of art I would sell for several months.

The day of 9/11, I was in my gallery with a client who was looking at a large work for purchase. It was a Tuesday and the gallery was closed to the public. We decided I would bring the artwork over to his home to see if it might work and fit in the space he had in mind. My phone was ringing the entire time I was meeting with him, which was unusual, and I turned off the ringer. He left, and I wrapped the artwork, got my van, loaded the piece, and took it over to his home.

When I got there, he asked if I had spoken to anyone or had turned on the news since he had been in the gallery. I said "no," as I had been busy preparing the artwork. He didn't say much after that and I noted to myself that his question was a little strange! He ended up purchasing the artwork that day and wrote me a check. I drove back to the gallery, parked my van, collected my things and went home, feeling elated and excited that I had just sold my second largest piece since opening a few months earlier. I was happy knowing things were going in the right direction with my business. I had just created a financial opportunity to move ahead and was to write a check to an artist, so they too could move ahead!

When I got back to the gallery the phone started ringing again. I picked it up and it was my mom who told me what had happened in New York and that my neighborhood, the historic district of Washington Square, Philadelphia, was a potential terrorist target and I should get out immediately.

I left my office that day and walked into a new America, one in which my business would take months and months to recover financially. I had already learned two important business lessons: first, there is typically a sales cycle that occurs throughout the year; second, the reality of the business world is inseparable from the economy and how people are feeling, whether it is fearful or optimistic, and which is dependent upon what is happening in our world and to a great degree in the stock market. These factors typically have a greater impact on new or younger businesses that don't have capital or large client lists and are still working on name recognition, as I was at that time. I was learning very quickly that it is important to know what business season you are in, whether you are an artist or a business owner, so you can make decisions and also be prepared.

Although the circumstances post 9/11 were challenging to me financially and devastating to our country, I still had a deep purpose, a vision and a desire to succeed which drove me forward and continued to create my success. I worked more hours and worked harder than ever at this time to forge new relationships and partnerships and to curate exhibitions that would impact the community.

The artists were also by my side creating new works and working hard in their studios to contribute and add value to the gallery program while deepening their artistic practice.

In looking back, part of my current success and happiness is knowing all the hurdles I had to clear to keep going to the next level. I was tested many times the first few years, and I continue to challenge and test myself and the artists with whom I constantly work. I was aware of the statistics for the number of galleries that open and close within their first year and overall in the first ten years. The longer I stayed open and worked on my passion as a gallery owner and curator, the more I was committed to the entire process of creating a thriving business. I had gone through several recessions, real estate purchases and other things that would set me back financially. I kept moving and adjusting to ensure that I would thrive.

Growth, forward momentum, making a difference and survival, these were the things that kept me going.

I was advising many of my artists at this time, who had second or third jobs, to be aware of their spending and minimize it and to not quit their day jobs. I told them to ignore the hype and negativity in the media, to stay focused and on course with their studio practices and not to be fearful. We were on a hero's journey, on an adventure, winning victories and changing and transforming in the process.

Part of creating a career as a creative is knowing what you want in your career and your life. Knowing what makes you happy. Seeing the vision for your career and your life in the arts as clearly as you can make it so you can begin to create it. This is the foundation of a successful career and will help you know what to focus on and pursue. I can't tell you how many creatives I meet that are just operating in survival mode. They are miserable, drained, afraid and full of self-doubt about their talent. Their daily thoughts are not focused on their art but on concern for whether they can keep going. They are not able to focus on goals and dreams as they are operating day to day and paying their bills so they can buy some supplies and keep the cycle going.

Artists and creatives are visual, auditory and sensory people. They see and hear clearly; they feel and think deeply. I have worked with artists to tap into this power to see, hear, and to create their future in advance. To focus on what they want and not on what they don't want.

I recently did a visioning exercise with a painter. I asked the artist to close her eyes, to get clear and imagine the perfect life and career she wanted.

This is the vision that came out of it:

"I see myself with a smile on my face and stepping into my studio which is a beautiful sun-filled space not too far from my home. There are 4 giant white walls in this studio in which I have 5 large canvases stretched and hanging. I just secured two large commissions which I finished, and they are getting picked up in a week after they are done drying.

The studio has a large area for works on paper where I have prints and works in a flat file and a few framed works hanging on the wall. It has a small kitchen area which means I can come into the studio early and stay as long I want to, as I have food, a bathroom and a sink. My life is great! I have paid off all of my graduate school debt and just paid off all of my credit card debt. I have money coming in every day and each week, so I am not only able to provide for my family but I save enough for my retirement, savings, and my two kids for when they want to go to college.

I am in the flow as I have two galleries representing me and both of them are consistently selling the work I give them and my prices have grown steadily each year. I am working on my first museum show and this will be the most amount of work and the largest work I have ever made! Each day I come to the studio, which feels like play and enjoyment to me, make my best work and go home to enjoy the rest of the day with my family.

I have checks coming to me every week and I have people coming to visit my studio and look at my work each week as well. My career is going exactly as I dreamed it would go when I set out to be a well-known professional artist. I am fully happy and satisfied and look forward to the magic and the new things that happen every day as they are always positive! I am excited for the vacation my family is about to take for ten days going hiking and then heading to a tropical beach to lay in the sun and play in the ocean. Life is great and my dreams continue to come true. I love what I have created!"

Amazing, right? If I described to you her career before this exercise, most would perceive it as a typical day in the life of a starving artist.

I am a believer in the idea of creating your future in advance, of creating your vision and creating your dreams. I have used this in all areas of my life, including growing my business and the types of clients I wanted to work with. On a personal level, I even used the visioning exercise to imagine the type of husband I wanted in my life. I wrote it down, read it and reflected on it regularly. My old model was to be organic and let things happen. I thought going with the flow was allowing myself to be creative. After talking to a high-achieving business coach, he likened my "go with the flow attitude" as a pinball hitting anything it would come into contact with and bouncing on the next thing to hit. Once I figured out how to be intentional and specific, many things shifted for me.

The first steps are to think about your dreams and what you want in any area in which you want to grow or to have more. Write them down, read them weekly, and start stepping into your future. Make them as clear, specific and as vivid as you can. Imagine yourself as an architect giving specific instructions to a builder to build your dream home. To do this effectively you need to be clear, thorough and paint the picture metaphorically speaking on what every detail of your home inside and outside will look like! In creating the ideal vision of your career and your life it is best to make it as clear as possible.

I can tell you from how my dreams have come true that it will happen. This is one of the first and most important steps needed to make it happen. Get the dream out of your head, get your words down on paper, get your voice heard, and start the process!

ACTION STEPS:

- Spend some time thinking about and then writing down what makes you happy. What are things you do with your career that bring you the greatest joy? How can you spend more time doing them?

- What have been the toughest one or two times in your career? How did you keep going? Remind yourself and come up with a mantra to match, such as: "Growth, forward momentum and making a difference create my success every day." Post it where you might see it often, such as on the bathroom mirror, on a studio or work space wall, or in your car.

- Utilizing the visioning exercise above, sit down, close your eyes and imagine your perfect career and life. Make it as visually rich and stimulating as you can. Use all of your senses and add anything that feels right. You can turn on your phone and record it as you go. When you are done, transcribe it on paper and read it often!

KEY TAKEAWAYS:

- For many, making a living from their art is as much a dream as it is inaccessible.
- The difference between success and giving up is possessing enough passion and drive.
- The starting point for being successful and happy with a career as an artist is to dream big.

Case Study:

The A-List Choreographer Who Built A Successful Business That Makes Him Happy On His Own Terms

If you are familiar with the world of dance—its choreographers, directors, dancers and ballet companies, chances are you have heard of Matthew Neenan. And if you live or work in or near Philadelphia, chances are you have heard of an incredible dance company that Matthew and his good friend Christine Cox founded in 2005 called BalletX.

Born in Boston, Matthew started dancing at 4 years old after being dragged to ballet classes with his two older sisters who attended the Boston Ballet School. Already at the age of 4, he knew that this was a world he wanted to be in, and as he grew older so too did his vision and clarity about what he wanted to do to continue to grow and propel him forward in the dance world. When Matthew was fourteen, he moved to New York where he attended The LaGuardia High School of the Performing Arts and The School of American Ballet. He moved to Philadelphia when he was nineteen and joined the Pennsylvania Ballet (one of his sisters was also in the company).

Matthew moved to Philadelphia at a time when the city was still emerging as the place for the arts it has become today. He intended to stay for two or three years, enjoying the more relaxed atmosphere of Philadelphia, being with his sister, and being in a smaller dance company (compared to the New York City Ballet).

Relatively soon, three years into his tenure with the Pennsylvania Ballet, he started choreographing. The director at the time, Roy Kaiser, gave Matthew an unrestricted opportunity to develop his work. For Matthew, this was another pivotal moment; he was beginning to achieve some of the career advancement he had imagined for himself when he was just 11 years old. This also kept him in Philadelphia where he then worked on a major project called "Shut Up and Dance" (a project that benefits MANNA). His years of involvement with this project helped him significantly to develop his choreography.

Thereafter he worked on a piece called "The Carlyle Project" by Barbara Weisberger, the founder of the Pennsylvania Ballet, while also doing similar small projects that kept him evolving in his career. During this time, he was also in discussions with his friend Christine Cox and other dancers about doing something during their summer layoff, and they decided to form a company called Phrenic New Ballet. There were five of them and they decided to just forge ahead. They worked on this project for five years after which time Matthew and Christine developed it into BalletX.

Did Matthew know at 17 or 18 that he was going to start a Ballet company at 25 years old? Not at all. He set his sights on becoming a great dancer and thought maybe he would do a little choreography as well. Hard work, being with the right people at the right time, and taking risks all helped him to keep evolving professionally. He co-founded BalletX in his 30s, and the move caused concern among people who cared about him; they worried about how hard it would be, about the stress of working in the circumstances most creatives face, which include being a 'starving artist' and the constant prospect of failing. Matthew felt at the time that if BalletX didn't work out or if he and Christine decided not to do it anymore then it would be ok as "no one died". That attitude kept them going during the initial uncertainty and the crazy schedule of dancing with both the Pennsylvania Ballet and BalletX, and doing everything to get a dance company started and running.

Evolution is a funny thing, and as he approached 40 years old, Matthew realized he needed to make a change, although he was not sure how he would accomplish it. He was being hired to choreograph around the United States, was doing research in New Zealand while working with a composer there, and was being pulled in multiple directions with a lot of responsibility. He was realizing that his passion was choreography and creating, not running the daily operations of a business and making the many important decisions necessary to running BalletX. He was realizing he needed to make a move that would enable him to continue to create his career in ways that made him happy. It was time for his next evolution, which meant not living his 40s in the same way he had lived his 30s.

In 2013, Matthew decided to step away from BalletX, from some of the business work that came with the responsibility of being a partner in a dance company, while he continued on his creative path of accepting commissions, doing choreography and the passion projects that stimulated him as an individual artist.

One thing that Matthew started doing as a young dancer that helped him become financially successful (and helped him later make moves advantageous to his career) was to put aside 10-50% of the money he made into a savings account and into investment accounts. If he made $1,000, he would take $100.00, buy a nice pair of jeans or something he needed, pay a few bills, and put the rest into savings and investments. This helped his money grow exponentially early on and enabled him to take advantage of certain opportunities or go places where he might have to spend a little extra money.

Early on in his career, Matthew accepted most projects that came his way. Now he can be more thoughtful or intuitive in making decisions about whether or not to accept a project. One factor he considers is if an opportunity will grow his network, put him in front of different people and give him the chance to make a creative contribution and make a difference for a group of people. He recently said yes to becoming the co-director of Jacob's Pillow, a two-week program in the Berkshires; one of the deciding factors was the opportunity to interact with and get to know A-list young dancers who are the future of the art form. Although he knew it would be a lot of work and challenging, he felt the opportunity to participate in such a situation would be tremendous for him artistically, professionally and personally.

In talking about recent projects with the New York City Ballet and the Pacific Northwest Ballet, he said: "Some choreographers even [those] who are in this program with me ... they're in their early 30s and they did their first piece and bam, every company's hiring them. That didn't happen with me. So, it's been a real progression. I didn't get my first commission outside Philly 'till after almost seven or eight years choreographing. And then it happened, and then a little more, and a little more. And now [there are] these bigger companies with bigger budgets. And so, I really appreciate it."

Matthew continues to grow every year, to make leaps and

bounds of evolution every ten years by understanding what makes him happy and following the path of that happiness while planning for the future. Through the sustained effort, persistence and clarity he has put into his career, he found the freedom to play in the work about which he is passionate, and thus has become a role model for many creatives.

2. The Perceived Reality

HAVE YOU EVER thought about why artists struggle and where their struggle starts?

I put a lot of thought into this, after I graduated, analyzing the idea of the 'starving artist'; while also having my own struggles at that time, trying to stay in the industry. For many artists, a similar struggle starts while they're in college. They might be a dancer, writer, painter or musician in college and only focused on their schoolwork and thinking about getting through college. Some people have to get a job to pay for books and expenses. Many artists will opt to go to graduate school, and once they get accepted, the reality kicks in: it's expensive. Of course, they should have known this already from the cost of schooling. But, for some, there is the idea that 'being famous' or well-known will take care of the bills. Also, a lot of creatives feel that worrying about money and bills will inhibit their creativity.

Secondly, being in graduate school is incredibly time consuming. Creatives can spend another two to three years really immersed in trying to figure out both how to have side jobs to pay for their food and expenses and how to give their full focus to graduate school.

The reality is that the whole process of learning the craft is incredibly time consuming. It becomes a struggle balancing this learning with earning enough to support themselves through the process.

They graduate with a degree, and then their new life chapter kicks in.

"Oh gosh. Okay, I just spent the last six years focused on learning how to make art. Now I have to figure out how I'm going to get my artwork out there, how I'm going to start making money from it, and how I'm going to connect with art patrons and a gallery. What am I going to do for work and how am I going to get a job? And how am I going to pay my bills?"

This struggle begins in undergrad or graduate programs where some creatives spend more time and money honing their craft. Most of these programs across the US and abroad are solely focused on their academic curriculum. Naturally, they prepare creatives about how to make their art formally and how to think about making art. There is a lot of critique, a lot of time spent on process and content, but, in fact, schools don't cover the business of art and how to make a living once you leave the four walls of the institution. What do creatives do at that point? This is really where their struggle intensifies.

We have these amazing and well-trained creatives coming into the marketplace, full of the vigor and optimism that they are going to 'make it' in the art world. Often, not long after that, doubt starts creeping in.

There is a common misperception about being a creative, and

even about being a gallery owner; it is the idea of 'build it and they will come'. It's sometimes thought that if you make something, if you do something, and if you put it out there, people are just going to show up, support it and buy it. To me, this is a myth about being creative. I have watched this phenomenon in the gallery world where well-intentioned people, without a business background in the arts, have the perception that opening a gallery is a matter of finding a space, painting the walls white, opening your doors with some exhibition of great art, and people will just come along to buy it. These people are often out of business in one to three years, and the same goes for professional artists.

A 2016 report titled *Creativity Connects: Trends and Conditions Affecting U.S. Artists* (National Endowment for the Arts 2016) summarized the situation as follows: "Making a living as an artist has never been easy, but broader economic trends such as rising costs of living, greater income inequality, high levels of debt, and insufficient protections for "gig economy" workers are putting increasing pressure on artists' livelihoods. Artists also face unique challenges in accessing and aggregating capital to propel their businesses and build sustainable lives."

Having a degree and knowing how to make great art, having a studio, even having a gallery working with you, does not necessarily translate into people showing up, knowing who you are and being compelled to buy your work.

So, the reality kicks in for a lot of artists after they come out of school with their degree in hand. They get their studio. They're in their studio making this great art they just learned how to make, and then start to think: "*Oh gosh. Where is everybody?*

How do I get people here to look at this?"

Maybe they have an open studio or a couple of people come by to look at their artwork, or they reach out to a gallery and they still don't have success. When they can't get into a gallery, they can't sell their art. And that's when more doubt occurs.

"Can I really do this? Is my art actually good enough to sell? Do people even understand what I'm trying to make? Where do I fit in to the art marketplace? And can I be a professional artist?"

These doubts can really cripple artists and cause them to retreat and withdraw. Some of them fall into real depression about this, which may cause them to actually stop making their art. Often times, they have to get one or two or several jobs to pay the bills, which means that now they're in a cycle of having to focus on bill paying, which takes away from their creativity and also takes away from the time they have in the studio to make their art.

The self-doubt can be incredibly crippling to artists at this stage in their career, because now they are facing public and professional rejection; again, this is not taught as a subject in school.

One of the stories common among creatives, that I have heard frequently, is that often they will work very hard for years with no results and no income. They will spend money on art supplies or rent for a workspace and even money to get their website up and running. Some creatives, like musicians and dancers, have to spend money to travel and to publicize their name, and still they continue to struggle with rejection and no money. They are not always equipped to deal with this.

This is the reality for many artists starting out. There are more ways than ever to get their art into the world, so it can be bewildering simply knowing where to best share their output. The normal education system doesn't prepare them for this situation.

I have seen this situation produce low self-esteem, even sometimes leading to desperation or cynicism. The self-confidence of some artists is affected by having the validity of their art questioned, and this can produce fear. I have seen artists stop applying for opportunities and stop getting their work out into the public because of this. They stop meeting with galleries, which can really halt them in their tracks and make them rationalize why their work is being rejected. These rationalizations can range from

"I'm just not good enough. I can't really make it"

to

"No one really understands me and my art. I'm making the art that I want to make, but no one really understands it, so it's really not my problem that people can't connect with what I'm making."

All this contributes to creating a cycle of negativity that can really hold artists back professionally.

A statistic published in a Philadelphia arts newspaper that I read in around 2004 indicated that after one to five years of paying for and getting a graduate degree, only 7% of artists coming out of a graduate program were actually still in the field, making and selling their art. That's just for Masters of Fine Arts students who have received their degree. When you think of the investment of money and time involved, this is a startling statistic! According to statistics, most of these artist graduates leave the field completely. A more recent report published in 2012 by the Census Bureau's American Community Survey (ACS) reported that: "Out of 2 million arts graduates nationally, only 10 percent, or 200,000 people, make their primary earnings as working artists."

Artists who make it over this one to five-year time hurdle, and who are still in the industry, will often, as I have witnessed, then take on a large amount of credit card debt. This is in addition to any school loans they have accumulated. Some of them are still feeling optimistic that at some point they're going to make it, but they are living from paycheck to paycheck.

While running a commercial gallery for the past 18 years, I have met a lot of artists who have upwards of $100,000 in debt, accumulated in just the first couple years after they finish school. They end up in a cycle of paying down very little and then accruing more debt through time.

There is not a comprehensive enough discussion in our culture around debt, cycles of success in the art market, and the reality of how many artists actually 'make it' and make a living as an artist. Creatives are not taught about the business side of the art world, perhaps because it could cause them to opt to not get their degrees, and schools would lose revenue or even go out of business.

Before I opened my gallery, I had the opportunity to decide to go to graduate school or to continue doing art consulting. I remember sitting down and calculating my current college student loan debt, which was close to $30,000 at the time, and then how much it would cost me to go to two years of graduate school to get an MFA from an Ivy League program.

I figured I would leave that MFA program with about $50,000 to $60,000 of student loan debt, and I calculated that by the time I graduated, I would be nearly $100,000 in debt. That to me was daunting. Then I started to work out how much art would I have to sell. I reflected on what would I have to do to become well-known enough to sell that art, and how long it would take me to do so. Back then, I figured that I would be in debt for at least 10 to 15 years, and that also, during that time, maybe I would also try to buy a house, have a family, all of which would accumulate even more debt.

At the same time, I still had the desire to go to school and get to the next level in the industry making art. So, I decided that I would go for it. Well, I ended up going to grad school for one week. I dropped out after one week because I realized I didn't know if I was going to make it. I didn't want to put the work into the studio process after all, and I was more interested in my art consulting business which I was running at the time. I knew I couldn't do both well; the latter would accumulate money and the former would accumulate debt.

I made a very deliberate decision, having calculated the debt that I probably would accrue, not to continue with graduate school and not to follow the path of being a working artist. This was a conscious choice for me, but a lot of artists are deeply driven, deeply passionate, very optimistic and confident that, once they enter graduate school, they're going to make it after they graduate.

There are enough examples historically and in the contemporary marketplace that support this optimism and confidence, but the reality is that, as I have said, artists are not taught anything about money in school. They're not taught about marketing and no one talks to them, including the professors that are teaching in these graduate programs, about their own circumstances of trying to be a working artist, pay off debt, and make it in the marketplace.

Another common assumption in our culture now is that a person can choose a famous artist who has made it, compare themselves to this artist, and imitate their behavior thinking that thereby they can make it too.

There is a lot of 'comparisonitis' in the art world and in our culture overall. I would say again that I believe it starts in college and graduate school when artists are surrounded by their peers. They're looking at other artists' artworks. They're also surrounded by more accomplished professors, and some people who have made it in the marketplace, and so they might start to emulate their teachers and their professors.

What I've found often with artists coming out of graduate school is that, even though most of them have a vision and have a solid body of work, they still have not found their authentic voice as an artist, because they're often trying to emulate or compare themselves to other artists. They have been trained in the style of a school's program, and it can be challenging in this environment to find their own creativity. Sometimes they end up creating the same kind of work these other artists are making.

It can take time to find your authentic and true voice, whether it is as an artist, writer or musician. You enter a new level of reality when you actually start making work that's your own, that's unique, and that develops into a viable kind of artwork to make in the marketplace.

Thus, even with the 7% of artists that do make it after school, it is somewhat inevitable that 93% of them are going to fall down this 'rabbit hole' and lose their way.

Sadly, many of these artists end of becoming hobbyists and have another career to earn their livelihood; art becomes a distant dream they once had. I can't tell you how many artists I meet in their 40's and 50's who tell me a similar story. They only paint when they have time and don't really consider it a career or a calling anymore. Some of them dream that they'll get back to being an artist after retirement or when they have some more money, which is often a great challenge.

As most of us get older, we have more expenses. We have debt that comes with families and kids, cars and mortgages. So, at some point the dream gets further and further away from an artist. Sometimes they're able to revive it but in most cases they're not; it becomes simply a hobby and something they know how to do really well.

ACTION STEPS:

⊚ We have all the answers inside of us already. We just have to ask the right question and let the answer come to us, hear it and then take action. Take out a journal, notebook or a piece of paper, ask yourself the following questions and then answer them:

- Am I thriving or struggling in my creative career?
- When did it start?
- How do I feel about where I currently am?
- What are three things I can do to turn it around?
- Who can you invite to your studio or to see your creative work whom you have always wanted to see your work? Write down three names and today email or call them with an enthusiastic and heartfelt invitation.
- Is there part of your creative dream that you have let die or one that you know you are not allowing to thrive? Write down what it is. What is one step you can take to revive it or to allow it to come back into your life? Do it!

KEY TAKEAWAYS:

- Struggle is a reality for many artists when they start out.
- Expenses, bills, limited time to make art and the realities of modern life often kick in.
- It can be unwise to compare yourself with others and not find your own unique path.

Case Study:

The Musician Who Followed His True North And Stayed True To His Voice

Christopher Sean Powell, also known as Pow Pow, Pay Pow and Powersati, is an accomplished musician, composer and song writer, producer, beat-maker, performer, teacher and scholar living in Philadelphia. Born in New Jersey, Chris moved to NY for a year after he graduated from high school, to immerse himself in the music scene and to begin fulfilling his dream of playing drums in a band and touring. He improved at his craft, started playing keyboards and writing music; eventually he began to produce records and got involved with electronic music. He has produced numerous albums, toured, signed with a record label, and experienced many levels of success in the music business.

For the past twenty years, Chris has collaborated, recorded and toured worldwide with a diverse spectrum of artists and musicians including The Sun Ra Arkestra, Yoko Ono, and Modest Mouse. He has also had success in getting his music into other mediums, including advertising and television. He is also creating instruments for NYC/Philly based synthesizer company Critter & Guitari's Organelle keyboard. Chris's experience as a musician and engineer is helping this company to produce competitive products that will position it at the next level in a niche market.

Like most creative fields, the music industry is competitive, tough to break into and have commercial success in, and not an easy industry in which to remain and sustain a career over many years.

How then did Chris navigate these challenges to continue furthering his success as a musician and artist? As he explained: "I would never go out to bars and talk about what I wanted to do. I would be in the studio working on it and doing it."

Chris began this practice early in the study of his drum craft, which allowed him to develop his expertise. He spent countless hours practicing, experimenting, and working hard to develop his talent, as well as in trying new things and expanding his ideas. He also added to his knowledge base by studying electronic music and its technology. While he was on tour and traveling, he used his time wisely to study electronic music production and engineering and to use what he had learned to teach, lead workshops, record with other people, and to initiate other musical projects. With his constantly developing skillsets and portfolio, he kept on attracting more artistic projects and opportunities.

One big advance in his career occurred in 2008 when his previous band Man Man was asked to open for the critically-acclaimed band Modest Mouse. Chris performed in front of audiences of thousands of people each night, which greatly increased his following and expanded his fan base. Previously, in 2007, he had secured a record deal with Anti-Records. Both of these career advancements gave him the financial means to continue realizing the music projects and artistic goals he envisioned.

Chris did not have any illusions of easy fame or greatness when he started out. He knew that he had to work hard to develop his talent, that he needed to 'play the game' and put himself out there, to connect and network with people. It started with him moving to Philly (after an initial move to New York for a year) and following his passion for being a drummer, and then ten years of touring as he worked hard to achieve recognition and financial security. He wanted people to know he was not just a rock musician, so he made and released recordings of the other kinds of music and formats, including abstract work, with which he was involved. He created a website and promoted his complete repertoire of work, and all of this was before the current proliferation and use of social media. Because of this promotion and the recognition of his work, many of his current projects come from word of mouth and referrals.

"You have to play the game somewhat," Chris says. "Over the years, I've known a bunch of brilliant musicians who would just blow me away as far as what they would come up with in their creative output and the things they would do but they basically refused to play the game...They didn't really care about doing interviews, they didn't care about and weren't really worried about promoting what they were doing. And sure enough, the opportunities end up not being there. You have to be able to talk about what you do and promote what you do and put yourself out there."

Many creatives are challenged by 'comparisonitis,' a condition exacerbated by how abundantly available and accessible other creative work is online and through social media.

Chris observes that "the most important thing is following whatever your true north is. These days, I think it's really, really easy to get bogged down and get hung up. Everyone's looking at their Instagram feeds and other stuff, and I think it's really easy these days to quickly compare what you're doing to all the other stuff out there."

Being authentically yourself, true to your own voice and to what you are trying to say has been a constant of Chris's philosophy. "For me," he explains, "the most important thing was to just keep working and to make sure that I was really trying to get my voice. To really just try and craft my voice...Everyone has something to say, and I think if you're genuine in a way, it becomes really easy to try and communicate that and connect to other people with that. And I never had a hard time being enthusiastic about that."

Chris maintains being successful in the music industry by doing what he has always done: doing the hard work, promoting himself, and seeking the ideas and skills to extend and expand his craft. He is teaching, leading workshops, consulting for various businesses, creating music for television and brands, along with, of course, pursuing his own musical projects.

To sum up the creative experience and purpose of his work as a musician and in the music industry, Chris said: "I just think music is magic and to be able to communicate that with people...[Just] to be able to share that magic with people, I think that's the most exciting thing about all of this. Music is life."

3. Out of the 'Rabbit Hole'

ARE YOU STUCK down a 'rabbit hole' in your life and in your career, in which your dreams of where you wanted to go have still not happened for you?

Has more time passed you by since you got your graduate degree, in which you have not been able to get ahead in your payments and your debt has continued to accrue?

Are you part of the 93% or more that drifted away from a career in the arts after getting out of college and the older you get the smaller your dream becomes?

I remember when I declared my studio art/art history major in college at Bucknell University. Bucknell was not considered an art school as such, and still isn't. It was a great liberal arts college that was more focused on engineering, business and political science, with the Arts being the least chosen major. I was the only one of two graduating seniors in my class of 1992 with an BA in Studio Art/Art History.

When I told my parents what I was going to major in they were not very happy about my choice. They wanted me to think about education and teaching or management and business.

They argued for how expensive college was and that I needed to use my time and the opportunity wisely.

Although I knew they were right, I still could not fathom picking a major that I was not excited about and for which I didn't feel a sense of passion. I would spend hours and hours in the library at Bucknell, looking through art and art history books, and spend hours in the printmaking studios and painting studios. I fell in love with photography and the dark room, taking photos and developing them. I experimented with materials and how to expand the medium. I spent a lot of time observing students, professors and college life and was stimulated by my 'art in the dark' courses and trips to New York, where we learned about living artists. The more I learned, the more I wanted to express myself through art making. I realized I could talk about sexism and racism through art making, and about all the things I was seeing, as a young college student, for which progress was needed in our culture. The thought of giving all of that up or putting it to the side, while I pursued education and teaching, did not seem authentic to me. I intuitively knew it would set me up for identity issues later on in my life.

Who was I listening to when deciding how I wanted my life and career to go? Was it me and my needs or my parents' practicality or the practicalities of the greater marketplace?

I decided to stay my course and listen to the part of me that told me to get a job in the art industry. Over the next four years of college, I spent each semester working in the college gallery, as a line cook at one of the eateries, and doing design and publicity work for the theater. In addition, I spent the summers of each of my first three years of college working several jobs in

New York; one was a non-paying job in a particular area of the arts, while the others were paying jobs. At the time, though, this was a practical strategy, as I had food, books, clothing and a car to pay for. It gave my resume an edge that my other young peers and competitors did not have. When I graduated, my resume included six years' worth of different job experiences and references.

My college resume and all of my summer jobs in the arts gave me an advantage in work experience, clarity about what I wanted to do and didn't want to do, and connections to get my foot in the door. It landed me my first job in a competitive gallery in New York. I was observing businesses and the industry in action. I was starting to notice, as I worked with them, where business owners were struggling and falling short. I noticed how professional artists were often poor and miserable, although many of them were incredibly talented.

A certain mindset of creatives started to appear to me, as I spent countless hours in artists' studios, at openings working in galleries, and seeing the results of exhibitions that took a lot of hard work and planning.

When I worked in a startup gallery in Philadelphia, and started to practice and put into action what I had learned and experienced over many years, it was my final tipping point. It was the reality check that I needed to give me my final push into starting my own consulting business and shortly thereafter my own gallery. I was fitting into the paradigm about which my smart and loving parents had expressed concern seven years prior, in which I would become a 'starving artist' and have an incredibly difficult life.

At the time, I was nearly $50,000 in debt, spread between student loans and credit card bills, I was barely scraping by and living paycheck to paycheck. I was getting paid what amounted to just over $7.50/hr. working in a gallery and made a little more in my second job as a teacher-aid.

The writing was on the wall for me. But at the time, I kept most of these struggles to myself.

In an act of frustration, I asked myself if anyone was making money in the arts, which led me on an exploration to identify who the moneymakers were and to see if I could figure out how to make a shift from where I was at financially into making more money in the arts.

After a few months of this exploration and assessing the industry, I read a book by Michael E. Gerber, *The E-Myth: Why Most Businesses Don't Work and What to Do About It* (Ballinger 1985), that changed my thinking. I had gone into the business section of a bookstore and picked out the smallest book I could find. I had my answer: I needed to be an 'owner' and open my own business.

What I have learned, observed and experienced, since 1996 when I entered the art world, is that there is a mindset certain artists and creatives possess. This mindset might serve them well in their creative practice. It might help them when experiencing rejection, fear or dismay about the industry, but it will not serve them well in building a sustainable, successful and thriving career in the arts.

When we are in college or in graduate school perfecting our craft and skills, no one is teaching us about mindsets for success or how to manage and think about debt, expenses or money. There isn't a focus in college or graduate school on how to market yourself as a creative and how successfully get your work into the marketplace. It is essential that you craft experiences, and a life resume, that will put you in touch with mentors, movers and shakers that can help transform your life and your career. In fact, what I came to realize was that many of the professors working in the Universities were struggling themselves; which is why they needed the teaching paycheck to sustain their own lives as practicing artists.

I learned that nothing comes easy, but that with sustained vision, focus and clarity, as well as by taking baby steps every single day, it was possible to create an amazing career.

I learned about ways top CEOs run their businesses and their lives, by studying what they did and didn't do. I discovered how marketing professionals promote themselves by promoting their clients. I learned that the spiritually inclined focused on their energy first, which allowed their dreams and money to flow their way. I noticed that the most successful investors spent time on what they were investing in.

It was becoming clearer to me that an artist not only needed a vision for where they wanted to be but also some clarity and methodology for how they were going to get there.

To get out of any hole we are in, the first step is to stop digging any deeper. Not only must you observe your current predicament but also observe and be honest about what got you there in the first place. This process may be a little painful, but it is not about beating yourself up. It is about identifying your current truth and reality so that you don't make the same mistakes again and again.

The next step is to spend time writing down your vision to strengthen your clarity. It is not, at this point, about worrying if it will ever happen. It is about creating the vision you want to live into and fulfill.

In 2001, when I decided to open my gallery, I had a financial vision for my life and a vision for my career based on having lived and experienced what I did not want during the previous five years. From this, I created what I did want. I wanted to sell and exhibit works that I believed in, that were amazing to me, and to work with great artists. I also wanted to be a millionaire and make the most money I could make, end the 'starving artist' syndrome in my life, and to prove to myself that I could do it. I had no idea at that time if I would be successful, or if my idea and concept would be received by anyone.

What I did know was that I had nothing to lose. I was making the least amount of money I had ever made in my life (I was paid more in my college jobs). I also had a lot of debt. But I still had my dream of trying to follow my passion to be around art and be in the art market.

I put a stake in the ground and got in touch with my vision. I then took the next steps of setting some initial goals. Where my goals were in 2001 and where they are now is drastically different! My goals in 2001 were to stay in business for one year, not default on my business lease for the gallery space, support myself with my business each month, not take on any new debt and to do my best to create the best gallery I could at the time.

At 26 years old, these were simple and earnest goals.

I was finally moving in the right direction, orienting myself to the horizon I wanted to head towards and not down the rabbit hole I had been in.

I was getting back in touch with my passion for art and my industry. I had disconnected from the fear, frustration and isolation that I had found myself in before I made the decision to open my gallery.

I was taking action and making a lot of forward-moving steps at that time. The more I did the more I learned what I was good at, what I was not good at, and what I needed to learn. It was incredibly humbling and eye-opening for me to strike out and do this on my own. I had always observed what other business owners were not doing, as much as what they were doing. When the reality flooded in as to just how much I didn't know, it made me even more resolved to learn and succeed. Now I was not only accountable more than ever to myself, but also to the artists I had taken on representing in my business and whom I wanted to help achieve more professionally.

The action steps and my growth attitude at the time got me through an incredibly difficult first year and on the path to growing my vision for myself and the people around me.

ACTION STEPS:

- Go into your local bookstore and head to the Business section. Read some of the book titles, look at some of the cover art and intuitively pick out a book to purchase and read. Depending on how many pages and how fast or slow you read, schedule your time to read and commit to finishing the book within 2-3 weeks. Reflect on what you learned. What lessons can you apply to your business as an artist?

- Is there an area in your creative industry or business in which, if you learned a little more about it, it could lead to another revenue stream? For me, it was learning how to value and appraise art. I know of an author who became an expert at clearing writer's block. See if there is something you could learn now or that you are curious about, that will be positive for you later, and make a commitment to learn and possibly offer it as a service.

Take out a piece of paper and a pen, set your timer for 20 minutes and time yourself writing as fast as possible about:

- What is my current reality in every area of my life?
- What is my desired reality?
- Don't think. Just write and see what you learn when the timer goes off. If you are inspired, set your timer again for one hour and craft a vision of your dream life and career. When you are done, read it out loud and see how it feels. If it gets you excited, you are on the right path. Read it weekly, or even daily, to get inspired.

KEY TAKEAWAYS:

- Any hole we find ourselves in is ultimately of our own making.
- There comes a time when we have to stop digging.
- It is important to develop a vision for how you will achieve your vision itself.

Case Study:

The College Dropout Who Dug Himself Out of Debt and Created a Million-Dollar Business

Jake Ducey is a two-time published author with Penguin Books: *The Purpose Principles: How to Draw More Meaning into Your Life* (TarcherPerigree/Penguin 2015) and *Profit from Happiness: The Unity of Wealth, Work, and Personal Fulfillment* (TarcherPerigree/Penguin 2016). A leading speaker for his generation, he has been featured in TEDx Youth and has been hired by global corporations such as Nielsen and Accenture. As a leader, he has already inspired a great number of young people to seek meaningful career success and to make a difference in the world.

Jake was not always this successful. He had to carve his own path, much to the frustration of family and friends who wanted him to stay on the safe track of being a business major in college, playing beer pong and following the herd. At 19, when, in an economics class, he was told to "shut up and memorize your textbooks," he realized college was not best suited for him; he decided to drop out, travel the world, and write an inspirational book about his journey (which he self-published).

Jake then faced the challenge of how to get people to pay attention to his book and purchase it. He was told no thousands of times to his face and lost count on how many people ignored him. Through tenacity and practicing a mantra he picked up from Jack Canfield, ("When someone says no, you say next"). He eventually sold 10,000 books and caught the attention of Penguin Books which published his next two books.

Jake had moments in his journey that were frustrating, but he was committed to his vision of living his life on his own terms and creating the business and career he wanted. He asked himself many times if something was worth doing; he wanted to achieve as much as possible in his life, knowing the typical life expectancy is 72 ½ years. He observed that many people spend their entire lives doing things which aren't worth doing, only to find out at the end that it wasn't worth it. He was determined he would not be one of these people!

Jake started to attract more money into his life, and thus respecting money became part of his journey. Taking care of his money and eventually saving as much as 40% of his income would, he realized, be important to creating more wealth. This sometimes meant the short-term sacrifice of purchases for the long-term goal of creating more self-sufficiency and digging himself out of the financial hole he was in. He committed himself to never being in debt; by acting consistently, he was able to continually save money and thereby to create more freedom and success in his life. After establishing this foundation, he next asked himself: How do I attract more money, so that saving this percentage of my income is no longer a burden on me?

He asked himself, "How do I earn from 5K to 7K a month and more?"

He started setting smaller financial goals like saving 5K in 45 days. He began looking at what he was doing in his business from a more strategic perspective, economizing his time and expanding his vision of possibilities.

Jake believes in a person creating a vision for his or her life and career. He wrote down on paper a powerful vision for himself that he read repeatedly over many years. He dreamed of being a world-renowned thought leader making millions of dollars and inspiring millions of people.

By training himself to think the reality he wanted, through hard work, building a foundation and consistently growing his finances, Jake has already achieved his goals in eight short years! He did a million dollars in business last year; he has inspired and influenced millions of people around the world, as his popular YouTube channel attests.

Jake has learned—and now teaches others—that you can create the reality you want and the life you want to live. Just don't forget to dream big!

4. The Worth of Your Art

WHAT WAS QUICKLY becoming very clear to me in 2001, and contributed to my business growth the past eighteen years, is the need to have a vision and to take action to move towards that vision.

How many people make the time in our busy days and lives to really get in touch with our life vision? To understand what is working for us and what is not working. What we love and what we hate and then to figure out how to have more of what we love and eliminate what is not working for us. I still have my own challenges doing this every year and resist it. For me it can be easier to keep going through my current days as they are and often with the excuse "I don't have time to do this." What I have learned is that when I do take the time around this yearly exercise, I learn more about myself and come up with creative solutions to challenges and sometimes drop what is not working for me completely. It is what keeps me moving forward.

Since I enjoy my industry and my work, a lot of my career to me has been a series of interconnected dots that progress into what I believe are higher challenges and purposes. My gallery has led to art consulting, art consulting has led to doing more complicated and larger public art projects and I keep learning and growing throughout all of these progressive career steps that I continue to make.

We are living in a time in which more than ever people have the opportunity to create the life vision we would like; a part of this is having access to the stories of other people across the globe that can inspire and motivate us.

From 1999 to 2000, I started to question who was actually making money in the arts and also to question why I was not being paid more. At the time, my quandary was in part because I was an employee and not an owner. I was working in an industry that had minimum wage and caps on salaries. In addition, I was not working in a highly competitive art market that affected even further the pay range I could make.

I began to see and identify my personal value and the value of what I was bringing to the table. In one of my gallery jobs the owners were new to the gallery world which is why they wanted to hire me as at that point I had been in the industry eight years. Not only did I realize that I had to move into the 'owner' mode of my career, but that I also needed to grow my own personal worth. Working hard and being humble came naturally to me. But what didn't come so easily was seeing myself and valuing myself for what I was really worth and then realizing this in my career.

How does this connect to artists and creatives?

It is vital that we take responsibility for our own career. One of the areas in which an artist can start doing this early on is to value their art and price their artwork or services at the appropriate level. This is the cornerstone from which to construct a solid foundation. Many times, I see artists giving their artwork away, either for free or at too low of a price. Getting your art priced correctly is an essentially important step.

Why is pricing your art properly so important? It is important because it begins to lay your financial foundations as an artist. Secondly, the sheer act of putting a price tag on a piece of art establishes that it has worth and value in the marketplace. It begins to place an artist—say, out of graduate school and getting started, and moves them from just painting and making art to now establishing the worth of this work by setting a price for a particular piece of art. It has worth which will be established in the market-place.

It's one of the initial steps that many artists will take once they have a new piece or an entire body of work completed. Whether they're working by themselves without gallery representation or they have a gallery or manager working with them, very early on they'll start to establish price points for their art. The same applies to an author working with a publisher or self-publishing or a musician with an agent and label or going it alone.

One of the questions that artists often ask is: do you price a piece of art based on how many hours it took you to create it, the size of it or on what the market will stand?

There is no 'one size fits all' answer to this question. Sometimes artists try to price their art by the number of hours they've put into painting it, and sometimes this can work, if their painting process is not too laborious. For example, I work with an artist for who it takes six months to paint a painting; it's a little bit challenging for us to calculate his time, and what that might add up to over a six-month period of time. I think in this particular case it does not work.

There are also artists—and you find more of this methodology in Europe, who want to price their art based on the physical size of the actual piece. This almost values art work like real estate. They say, for example, "Well, if it's a 40 cm x 40 cm painting, then per centimeter, this is my price."

I've found this to be a little bit confusing. I think, in America, it's a little bit different and pricing is traditionally based on your position in the marketplace. Are you a new, young, emerging, unknown artist who is stepping into the market where you don't have a sales track record or any clients? If you haven't sold anything or you haven't sold much, your prices are going be at the level for an emerging artist.

Or, are you a more established artist that has had a couple exhibitions? You've been selling your work for a little while and now you're going to establish your price point at that level. Typically, by this time, such artists have galleries working with them and helping them to establish their pricing. Then there's the higher level of artist who may have been collected by museums. They might have exhibited in a higher-level gallery and the price points at that gallery drive their pricing.

It could even be driven by the marketplace the artist is showing in. For example, if you go to Chelsea in New York City, and walk into a typical gallery there, most artists have price points starting at $25,000, whether the artist is known or unknown. It is more based upon the New York marketplace, along with the gallery's overhead and expenses. It has nothing to do with the experience of the artist, quality of the work or some of the more tangible characteristics that drive the pricing of artworks.

If you go to another market, like Philadelphia (the one I've operated in for many years), and walk into a gallery on any given day, you're very unlikely to see a price point over $10,000. It's just a different level of artist and marketplace. So yes, pricing can be driven by the marketplace the artist is in.

Obviously, now we're just talking about art as in painting, drawing, or fine art, but pricing of one's art is a fairly similar process whether you are an emerging dancer, musician, writer or designer.

In most creative marketplaces, there's typically a going rate for the type of work that you're doing. It's really going to be based upon your experience and what a particular person, dance company or publisher might be willing to pay you for your work and time. I have worked with writers in my business who might want a flat fee of $300-$600 to write a 2000 word well-researched essay. At the higher end, I have paid top writers $5000-$6000 for that same number of words. Some of these writers are published authors or experts in their industry. They commanded these rates because of what they have created and what they are willing to work for. You are paying for their expertise and for their 'brand'.

The challenge early on is establishing your name and starting to establish the worth of your art, which hopefully will grow over time. I have also seen a lot of creatives make the mistake of over-pricing their art or their creative work. It's tough to go backwards and then reduce a price once you have established it. I'm always cautious with pricing.

My feeling is: why not build into the market slowly so you can keep growing and not lock yourself into a certain price point from where you can't really go backwards. It's difficult, as I said, once you've established a price to go backwards and reduce it. My method is: price consistently and continue to price up as you sell more art and as you get more recognition.

Sometimes you need to price higher based upon the materials that you're working with. If you're a sculptor and you're working in precious metals, like aluminum or some other material that has a higher cost associated with it, you might need to account for this in your price point. If you're a dancer or musician who is traveling and has hotel expenses, that is something that would have to be accounted for too.

Again, it's really a matter of who you are and where you're at, of whether you are emerging or you are established. It also depends around the managers, publishers and the business people around you and how they see your worth when helping you price your art or your services or your products.

It is quite common to come across artists who undervalue their work.

If an artist tells me that they're selling out of all the work they have in the studio, I have two thoughts. One, the art is really great and everyone wants to buy it, so it's good that it has sold out; and two, it's really good work but it's underpriced and people are aware of this, so they're going to grab it before it goes up in price.

I was recently working with someone who has sold out the last two bodies of work that she's made, and I had to tell her it was time for her to raise her prices. It didn't need to be a significant price raise, but enough so that she could start to earn more from each sale. Raising your prices is a key part of your growth, as your client base and your notoriety is increasing. They really go hand-in-hand. My client raised her prices by 10%, which made her price increase between $300-$800 for each work of art. Several months later, she was able to book a dream trip with her partner to Europe for ten days! She was very thankful to have had the advice and the push from me to increase her pricing. It can be scary when you are doing well to shift pricing, for fear of losing clients. Now she is on track to bring in more income, which was one of her goals.

There is a lot to learn and do as an artist besides learning the craft of your art and learning to be an artist in the marketplace. Part of the evolutionary journey is getting the right pricing and value for your art.

Early on, the challenge is that the cost of materials, or for other creatives the cost of time and travel and things they need to do to get themselves and their work out into the world, is often significant. Many creatives don't have patrons yet, and they don't have people buying yet, which adds to the challenge. They tend to set a reasonable price point coming into the market. When they make a sale, most of it goes toward paying their expenses. There's often a period of time in which they're still barely scraping by or breaking even. It can cost a lot to make a piece of art and to recover that cost with a profit once the art is sold. The evolution in becoming more successful centers in part around the sale of more art and earning more money which enables you to sustain your creative work.

Once you have established your work, once you have some business relations established and people that are managing you, representing you or publishing you, then typically you should have consistent money coming in. From that point, you can begin to apply more focus on your art making. That could take artists years to get to. In my program, I was selling work early on in my business but it took about five years before I started to really make a dent in yearly sales numbers for artists and before they could see the impact of that.

My advice to artists is to be patient and persistent in their endeavors. For some, it is a two, five or ten-year process to start 'making it.' I have also watched people give up before they have had time to gather momentum and become successful. I've seen artists coming out of graduate school who can't find a gallery. I've seen a classmate of these same artists land in a gallery and their career instantly skyrockets. In reality, it's all about being proactive, about getting out there and trying to establish your name and forging your business relationships with people. It is a chicken and egg situation though: to get people looking at your art, so that you are able to sell your own art, or to have others sell the art for you and have a steady source of income.

As I mentioned, one of the things that artists might contend with or experience is the assumption that everything comes for free or the expectation that their work, products or services should be free or inexpensive.

Any type of art form—writing, dance, fine art, composing music, takes time and has a worth. In the case of fine artists, there's a material cost involved in making that piece of art exist. I'm not a fan of artists giving their work away for free. This model is often pushed onto artists, the expectation that they're going to give their art away for free, or that they're going to work for free. Sometimes it's thought that they don't deserve the same rate of pay as someone else, because maybe they are doing something that they enjoy. I've worked really hard to make sure that artists get paid what they deserve.

What has helped recently is an artist's independent opportunity more than ever to show, sell and get their work out to a global marketplace using the Internet.

When I started my business in 2001, people still did not really understand the impact of a website on a business. We were still learning that having a website was important and that it was an extended business card. Now the Internet has become a place to trade and do business. Most of us shop online. Nobody knew then the impact that the Internet would have in the art world and it continues to evolve every year.

Artists entering the market now have a greater opportunity to sell and disseminate their work than ever before.

Of course, if an artist has a sense of guilt, or if they love doing their work so much that they see it as play as opposed to work, these attitudes can create a mindset whereby they perceive themselves as not worthy to receive money in exchange for something they love doing.

This mindset can ultimately hamper and hurt an artist's

progress and make it tough to devote more time to their creative endeavors.

This is a very common attitude I encounter in talking to and working with artists. I encourage artists to get in touch with what I call their money mindset. (Money mindset is simply how you think about money and then how that affects your life and career.) I think some of the best art gets made when artists are in this very playful, organic, spontaneous, passionate mode of making their art. Then the question is what happens when they're finished and now they have to get it out there?

What I've discovered for myself and a lot of creatives is that your money mindset or your thoughts about money and value really start in very early childhood. This is where we start learning about money. For example, in my family, my parents would often say to us: "Money doesn't grow on trees." There was this feeling of you had to be careful, you had to take care of your money, you had to use it wisely, as it doesn't come easy. I had to do a lot of work after I started my business to not carry on this mindset, and I had to reverse it in my mind. I told myself that paper money actually does grow on trees, to help me get in touch with the abundance mindset.

Many artists grow up with this lack-of-abundance mentality, which they translate into their own personal feelings about taking money in exchange for something they've produced. I like to do a deep dive with people and get them to pick apart their earliest memories of money, of what they heard repeatedly growing up. I ask what they witnessed in their families around the cycle of money; that is, how money was made, saved (or not saved) and utilized, which are part of parental/family mindsets

around money that are taught to children and passed on gen-
erationally.

ACTION STEPS:

Some key takeaways for any artist, writer, musician, dancer,
sculptor, who is studying and trying to establish their worth and
the worth of their art are:

- ⊙ Educate yourself about your industry and what the
  various rates are for creatives working in circumstances
  similar to yours. Whether just starting out or whether
  you've been in the field for five years, there are
  established criteria to use as a baseline from which to
  start.
- ⊙ Next, understand where you fit in the marketplace. You
  could talk to a mentor or someone in your industry
  to get their perspective on setting a price for your art
  or a value for your services. Then test the water in the
  marketplace and see what the response is.
- ⊙ Check if you are acting like the CEO of your own art or
  creative business. Where can you start being more a
  CEO and less an employee? Identify three things you
  can do and start doing them today!
- ⊙ Have you ever had someone knowledgeable take a
  look at how you are pricing your art, services or what
  you are selling or billing for creatively, and give you
  feedback? Find a professional that you admire and
  trust and ask them for some of their time to give you
  feedback. Are your works priced well? Are they priced
  too high or too low?
- ⊙ Do you know what your money mindset is? Write
  down your earliest memories regarding the subject of
  money. Do you remember any family memories of it?

> If you have some negative feelings or thoughts about money, write down the opposite mantra for yourself. Explore how you can switch your mindset.

KEY TAKEAWAYS:

- We can feel guilty getting paid for doing something we love.
- There is always worth in what we create.
- Every artwork has its price and its market.

Case Study:

The Worth of Your Art: Ryan McGinness

There are thousands of artists living and working in New York City and around the world who are trying to become known and create a successful art career. Not all of them are able to do this and thrive in a competitive industry. Ryan McGinness is an American artist, based in New York City, who has had a prolific career and has managed to develop and sustain it on his own terms. Born of "hippie" parents who encouraged him at a young age to have ideals beyond money and financial success, McGinness believes that art is priceless and that no price will ever be too high for a work of art.

Known for his original and extensive vocabulary of graphic drawings which use the visual language of public signage, corporate logos, and contemporary iconography; he also creates paintings, sculptures, and environments. He is interested in assuming the power of this anonymous aesthetic in order to produce and to share his personal expressions. His work is in the permanent public collections of the Museum of Modern Art, Virginia Museum of Fine Arts, Museum of Contemporary Art San Diego, Cincinnati Art Museum, MUSAC in Spain, and the Misumi Collection in Japan.

McGinness grew up in the surf-and-skate culture of Virginia Beach, Virginia, and its influence is visible in much of his work. Enterprising and creative at a young age, he sold his first work of art in sixth grade to an art teacher for $40.00, and since then he has come a long way. McGinness' works command between 100-200K, and his installations have earned him more than 600K.

One of Ryan's first business ventures, when he was just twelve years old, was to write letters to surf-and-skate companies seeking their 'sponsorship' for a skate event in Virginia Beach that he had organized. Companies responded by donating swag and skateboards that he gave out to attendees of the event. This was an early lesson in commerce and corporate sponsorship. He explains: "When I was growing up in Virginia Beach, I painted skateboards and t-shirts for my friends, and these objects were valued. Art was used to define what was cool, and assuming that power was intoxicating."

Early in his career, one of McGinness' main goals was to achieve the sustainability that would enable him just to carry on in his art-making. He is not an artist that chases money or even pays too much attention to it. He has a good accountant that helps him manage his finances and is incredibly organized; he plans out his exhibitions and projects one to five years in advance. Although he would say that money is not really on his radar, it is evident he is smart in how he manages his time and his money so as to allow himself the full creative freedom he needs to produce the works he is interested in making.

The very clear vision he has for his artwork is separate from his career sense, which develops in an organic way of its own and which he feels "is out of his control". He relies on his galleries and on art professionals to price and market his work, and to handle the business aspect so he can focus on his projects and creative processes. His projects often require several years to complete, and he often has multiple bodies of work in progress simultaneously, each of which can also take years to complete. He doesn't focus on career milestones as such, but on his work and planning it through to completion.

One key to McGinness' success as an artist is in his being very selective about who gets to sell his work and who gets to buy it. "As an artist," he explains, "every work of art you make is a share of stock in your career. So, in order to maintain as much control as possible, I've always tried to keep sales private and keep as much of my own stock. I want to avoid being a publicly traded company."

The success of his approach is evidenced by the museum and private acquisitions of his work, as well as by his public art projects and murals around the world. Having a great accountant, making lists to stay organized, combined with maintaining his high standards for the quality of his work and for who he chooses to manage it, have helped maintain McGinness as one of today's top collected and coveted artists. And as he iterated to me: "Art is priceless. No price will ever be too high."

5. The Two Paths

I HAVE BEEN in the art world since I graduated from college in 1996. I have spent time in the non-profit sector working at The Artists Space. I have worked for a commercial photographer in New York and have spent most of my time in artists' studios and working commercial gallery jobs. Together these gave me an early understanding of the gallery world and the artists operating in it.

Throughout those years, I came across artists who have a laissez-faire attitude, taking their time, not concerned about the industry, money or their place in it. I've also encountered artists who are proactive, who market themselves and their art and really take the 'going for it' path. I have also found artists who oscillate gracefully and tactically between these two paths.

There are many cultural myths around being a creative and being an artist, and most of us have heard of the 'starving artist' syndrome. We've heard how hard it is to 'make it.' In addition, with the Internet connecting us to people and their lives, we now have access to so many people around the globe and can see how they seem to be doing professionally. We might see artists who are selling well at auction, or publishing multiple books, or are famous choreographers being written up in the New York Times. There is more awareness now than ever in what is possible for a creative career.

Sometimes artists are attracted to being famous just for fame's sake. They see it as a validation of their work and they then take their eye off their work.

What I have observed is that creatives will begin their careers very optimistically and go for it with gusto. They are either going to keep snowballing that success, keep it gaining momentum or, if they have a lot of setbacks, they will sit back and keeping making art in the vain hope they will get discovered one day. This latter choice can result in them becoming a hobbyist for whom art is no longer their primary career. Art then becomes more of a secret passion they have or their hobby.

So, artists have a choice between this lesser path and the greater or higher path of really going for it, of being out there and being proactive. It is realistic to recognize that it's going to take a lot of sacrifice, some sweat and a lot of time invested. By consistently taking baby steps each day, an artist has more chance at some point of reaching a tipping point where they find their voice and their career mission.

There is also the possibility of alternating between these two paths in a conscious, mindful way.

This might involve taking a break, recharging, and then coming back into the market. Taking time away, and being mindful about it, does come with the territory. Many creatives take sabbaticals, go on retreats or work on a project for a year where they are off the grid. All creatives need time to regroup around ideas, and sometimes disappearing and then returning can really catapult them forward.

One creative that comes to mind is David Bowie who would step away for a while, and not do an album for a few years, and then come back with a brand-new persona. He had this amazing knack for choosing the persona that was right for the zeitgeist.

This strategy gave longevity to his career and a mechanism for maintaining brilliance and freshness. To me, it is important for artists to continue to evolve and change who they are in order to grow. There can be stagnation in continuing to make the same works over and over again each year and not to keep exploring.

Some artists can get stuck and comfortable when they have a formula for something that's worked and produced success for them in the past. It is natural for them to lock into the formula, but it is dangerous because over time the formula itself can become stagnant and start working against the artist who uses it. You can plateau, and then maybe go into decline. If this happens, it's a good tactic to step back again and reimagine and revision before moving ahead.

I was talking with a friend about writers having a nom de plume, such as the writer J.K. Rowling who wrote the Harry Potter series. She wanted to explore other genres such as writing detective novels and published books under another name, Robert Galbraith. The question is, can creatives have another persona who makes art in a slightly (or substantively) different way?

I have seen this quite often with musicians, designers and writers. On the art side of the industry, some artists will be compelled to explore other media such as video or sculpture in order to enhance their main creative practice which might be painting. Some of my favorite artists are working across genres. I believe this both strengthens their vision and enhances their creative spark.

Why not have a multiple personality and try something new? See how it feels and explore other paths.

In the Buddhist tradition, there is the concept of the Middle Way, which is a way that avoids and transcends extremes. I would characterize much of the art industry as, analogously, following a middle way or a path of moderation. The only path that is right is the path that you are being called to. How do you know what path you are on and what path you are being called to?

A lot of it is intuitive. Are you happy with the path you're on? Do you feel like you are being your best self or your most successful creative self? Are you making the work that you feel deeply called to make? Are you simply making the work that you know is going to sell and be a success in the marketplace? What type of work are you making? These types of questions call for an intuitive answer.

These are questions for which we might turn to our soul for guidance. Often, we can find answers to this type of question in our dreams or when out in nature for a walk or sometimes even in the shower!

In my work as a gallerist and curator, it has been important to me over the years to ask myself whether the work that I was being called to curate, and the artists who created it, resonated with me personally. As I went out and found them, I also found I was blessed with the radar to know if they were growing and evolving or if their art was stagnant. You can look at an artist's portfolio over time and see if they are evolving or just recycling the same artworks.

It can be a lifelong exploration for an artist to find their voice and discover what resonates with them. Getting to that point is not necessarily easy. Going to graduate school and taking time to only focus on your art is meant to give artists that clarity and vision and expose them to ideas and mentors, but it might not all click immediately. Patience and persistence are the keys here.

When you find your voice, you also find your passion and your uniqueness. That's a calling into the marketplace that we've all witnessed at some point, either with others or ourselves. When we see brilliant creatives standing there in the spotlight, we know that they have found themselves. They've found their zen-like creative peace and they're moving on their path.

Someone recently asked me about what success for creatives is predicated on. One, on how good you are at your art; and two, how good are you at non-core skills like getting in the zone, being intuitive, having the right mindset about money and some of its practicalities.

One of the questions for our time is who are the important creatives who will make history or impact the industry and our culture? In the Fine Arts, it is easier to go back in the history of Art and see the artists who were incredibly talented but who were ahead of their time. One that comes to mind is Van Gogh. His artistic talent is really not in question; however, he lived in the shadows and didn't really have opportunities to exhibit and have his talent recognized while he was alive.

It seems to me that what is more important these days is not necessarily your artistic talent but how good you are about being around the right people and putting yourself into a position to promote and exhibit yourself. There is some luck associated with this, but creatives these days are in a position to create their own luck, given how interconnected our world is. Both paths, the laissez-faire path and the pro-active path, are available. Which one do you want to take?

ACTION STEPS:

- Come up with a new personality for yourself, if you don't already have one. Give this personality a name and write down 2-4 things he/she would do that you might not be doing now. Is there a way to work any of this new personality into how you handle things currently?

- For example, Daring Kim. Daring Kim is vivacious, outgoing and LOVES talking to people. Her calendar is always booked up and her phone rings off the hook with people wanting her to come to events and be there with them. Is there a way to create a 'Daring Kim' or alter ego for yourself in real life?

- Schedule a 2-3 week 'time off' period to completely step away from your work. During this time do things differently. Read new books and go to places to re-inspire you. Keep a journal and write new ideas. Go to places you haven't been locally or plan a weekend trip away. At the end of this period, what can you bring back into your work with fresh ideas and fresh eyes?

- Is there an event or somewhere you can go to be around the right people or different people to gain exposure? Book something on your calendar this month in your area that you might not ever consider going to and see what the outcome is after you go. Did you meet someone new? Did you have an interesting conversation or get to share what you are doing creatively with someone that might have an impact?

KEY TAKEAWAYS:

- There always is a higher path.
- Taking the lesser path is sometimes wise and prudent.
- It's a good idea to allow the higher path to be shown to you.
- You can take both paths at the same time and find a middle way.

Case Study:

The Meditation Guide Who Thought He Was an Author

Tom was a successful author who, at the time this book was written, had published 16 books in 10 years. As an author however, his success was really in his prolific output and the range of his works and not necessarily his volume of sales. He had a loyal following, generally got 4 and 5 star reviews, but his books sold in the low thousands and some just in the low hundreds.

Being a generous and kind-hearted soul, many of his books provided a link whereby readers could sign up for free resources they could use to supplement their reading experience. Many of these resources were meditations. The prevailing marketing trend was to offer something for free in exchange for an email address. The idea being that you then upsell something of higher value to the compiled email list. The strategy was that 1000 emails sent would end up with 100 emails opened, 10 clicks and perhaps 1 sale. It was kind of a numbers game.

Just over 3 years ago, Tom found a new path by accident. More accurately, the path found him when he was approached by the publishing manager—an unexpected helper—from an app called Insight Timer. It was at the time, and continues to be now, the most popular free meditation app on the planet. Tom was asked if he would like to share one of his free meditations, which he willingly did.

He then forgot about it completely, for a month, until the publishing manager got back in touch. She asked him if he'd been looking at the feedback. He hadn't. So, he logged online and found that, in one month, the meditation that had previously been reaching a handful of people per month had had over 6,000 listens. More importantly, meditators reported it was the first meditation that totally helped to silence their mind chatter and how much they loved Tom's British accent and sense of humor.

Winding the clock forward to today, Tom has well over 2 million listens to his meditations and he has become one of the top 20 most popular meditation guides, out of over 3000, on the app. What's more, the app now has optional premium courses which generate a nice monthly income while Tom sleeps. Around 2000 people meditate with him each day, all without him having to lift a finger to find any of them. The market has come to him and, somewhat ironically, a fair number of them listen to a meditation and then track his website down and read his books. Some have even ended up as fee-paying clients for one-to-one mentoring.

So, what has Tom learned about his path? Rather than being an author who creates some nice meditations, he is an unexpected meditation guide, who has never been inside an ashram, who happens to write some rather nice books. Most importantly he learned that his storytelling ability works as well in audio as well as in print. His meditations are like short stories for the mind.

The story is not yet finished. Sixteen books ago, Tom started writing a novel that he has never published, as he always put his non-fiction and (ideally) sales-generating books first. Now that his meditations are providing a solid monthly income, he can take his foot off the gas and indulge in his long-suppressed passion and dream to be free to write fiction without worrying where the pay check is coming from!

6. A Smarter Plan

HAVE YOU EVER considered how important it is to have some sort of plan for your career?

It might seem obvious, when asked this question that, of course, it is important to have a career plan. Aside from graduating from a program, getting a studio and creating art in the studio, most artists do not have a career plan! Worse yet, some feel that planning goes against the grain of being a creative.

One of the problems people have is that they've only planned as far as the process of the creation of the work of art involves.

I've mentioned before that when you're in school, and studying, and learning your craft, the focus really is on the creative process. You are still finding your voice, learning the technicalities of what you're making and how to make the best work. What a lot of artists find, and what I've experienced, is that in school no one is talking about the day you step out of the school program and enter the real world. You're going to need to know how to market yourself. It is as important to connect with the right people, or what some people might call the gatekeepers in the creative fields. The real learning is about how to get creative jobs, how to secure a studio, how to think about your finances, how to sell your work and how to effectively go about the business of being a creative.

A savvy business person once asked me: what if someone doesn't want to do that? Can they just outsource the whole effort?

I would say for most creatives starting out that outsourcing is too expensive. From my own business experience I can share that, when I started my gallery in 2001, for several years, I did all the work by myself. After a year of doing my own bookkeeping and accounting, I realized that I needed someone else with better experience to do this for me, as it was incredibly time consuming. So that was the first thing I outsourced. It took me a couple years to be able to hire a gallery assistant, as I really didn't have the money for this, since I needed to pay my rent and fixed expenses. In the meantime, I would work with interns to help me do different things like marketing mailings. Looking back, I had to wonder: if I had paid even a part-time person to do some of the more tedious work that was not about business growth, would that have given me more time to work on my business instead of simply working in it? Could I have invested some of the money I was making in sales towards staffing instead of, say, towards advertising? These are the questions I continue to ask, as I keep growing my businesses and advising artists who are doing the same.

Most artists, when they come out of school, whether it's college or graduate school, have student loans and debt. The idea of spending more money to get help is a bit daunting for them. The idea of hiring people to do some of the work that they don't want to do is quite challenging. Sometimes people will make trades. I know artists who, for example, trade a painting for someone to do their taxes, or who paint a work of art for someone to do their bookkeeping or to handle photographing their work professionally.

I'm always encouraging creatives to recognize there's lots of younger people who are trying to get their foot in the door and intern for artists or be studio assistants. Heck, I worked without pay in New York for four summers in a row, spending 40 hours a week working for professionals to learn as much as I could. Doing 40 hours of data entry for an artist was incredibly helpful to them that summer, as was me picking up their dry cleaning, booking appointments, updating their website, and the other routine tasks I did.

In return, I got free lunches and coffee and got to meet people in the art world I would not otherwise have encountered. At the end of the summer, I had a kick butt letter of reference to add to my resume! In my own gallery business, I have gone on to hire two of my interns who were exceptional. So, do consider that if you do good work it is not necessarily for nothing.

If you are not sure how or why to outsource, find someone with complementary qualifications to yours who is eager to be in the industry. Look at their skill sets in advance and see if they are better situated to assume certain tasks for you. An intern or helper can help prepare stretchers or canvases, or help with things like building your mailing list, creating email broadcasts, helping you with social media marketing, updating your website or researching sales opportunities.

The question to ask yourself is where are you spending a lot of time doing tasks that need to get done but that don't necessarily bring in income. Running errands, stretching canvases and updating email lists strike me as the necessary things that need to happen but that don't have an immediate return on investment. I think these are some of the ways that people could creatively get some help. If I am interviewing someone for an internship position, I am very clear with them about what they will be asked to do to, and I let them decide if it is something they are ok with doing. My attitude during the 8 internships I had after I finished college was that the better an intern I was, the more likely I was to get good letters of reference and get asked to take on more responsibilities.

Some creatives I know use sites like fiverr.com, as both users and providers. You could either get something done for $5 or you could produce a service based on your artistic skills and generate that $5 for yourself. This could be a way to pull yourself up by your bootstraps and get your name out there. It is a great resource! I've actually used it for graphic design work, for presentation work and to format presentations.

Recently, I had a very large PowerPoint presentation to pull together and I guessed it was going to take me a full working day to complete. I figured that my time was better spent to pay someone else to do it and then I could add edits that might take me 15-20 minutes. Ultimately, with the right designer, it would end up looking better than if I did it myself. I spent just under one hour pulling together the images, text and order of it, setting up my account online and finding a great designer very quickly. I sent my clear instructions by email and the designer took over. I had a draft in my inbox the next morning. I emailed over a few quick edits and had my final document a few hours later. Total time for me to do this? 1 hour and 15 minutes. Total investment? $25. Time is money!

When I started my business in 2001, one of the things early on that scared me most was bookkeeping and taxes. I would read articles. I learned how to use QuickBooks. I was tracking my receipts, but I still didn't really like doing it. I ended up meeting with a bookkeeper who showed me the nuts and bolts of what I needed to track and how to do it. Once I learned this, I actually felt excited about it because I felt like I knew what I was doing. However, after one year of this I realized I was not that efficient with it and spent way too much time dealing with it, when there were more important business issues and opportunities that required my attention. I also was smart enough to realize accounting is such an important part of my business but not something I should be spending my time on each month and that there were probably things I was missing or not doing and that I should hand it over to a professional.

The most important thing is to focus precisely on what you like to do because that's where your passion lies. For most artists, it comes down to wanting to be in creation mode. They want to be in their dance studio, they want to be in their design lab. They want to be in their painting studio. They want to work on the creative work for which they have trained and that they love doing.

On the other side of this creativity is the practical business side. Many creatives end up having a hard time with things beyond making their artwork, such as making a sale, getting a grant, generating invoices, and actually asking for the money so they can get paid! They don't leave their art programs with a business degree in hand and often they are encountering these things for the first time.

There are many basic administrative functions to running a business, such as creating an invoice and having an invoice template, knowing if you need to bill sales tax on a sale, understanding what the client might be responsible for paying, or what the artist might be responsible for paying or how to negotiate this. There are a lot of basic business skills that we just don't learn in school, but that you encounter once you're thrown into an industry. Sometimes artists just run in the other direction. I've had artists I have worked with for whom it takes weeks to send an invoice. Part of it is they're afraid and they don't know how to do it. They don't want to take the time, so they're blocking their own flow of money coming to them because they're not sending out the invoice to get paid.

There is a smarter approach. It involves a monthly plan that includes devoting the majority of your time to creative tasks. This involves thinking about the month, week or the day ahead, and actually knowing how you are going to tackle it!

For artists, an important part of having a great plan, or a smarter plan, is to be able to plan their weeks and their daily schedules to make sure that they're tackling all the areas in their business that require their attention. The first thing I like to tell artists is that they should determine for each week how many hours they have available that week, outside of other family and job commitments, to work on their career. Just make a rough estimate to start with.

For example, some artists have a full-time job or a part-time job, so they have to schedule their art business time around this. The first question is: how many hours do you have in a week? For example, I just worked with an artist on creating her schedule. She determined that in a week she had 25 hours available to her when she wasn't teaching or commuting.

We looked at that 25 hours and then we split that time between her painting, writing, or studio time. Then we also split that time up between professional development time, where she was taking care of invoices, updating her website, following up with people that had emailed her, and looking for potential exhibitions and opportunities. Then there was also time scheduled to get out and go to events, to network with people, and try to be out in the community meeting people that either she would invite back to her studio or that she would connect with professionally to further relationships.

In that 25 hours, she decided that she would allocate 15 hours a week to her painting, five hours a week to professional development activities. Again, this could be updating her resume, doing marketing posts on social media, calling people back, looking for opportunities or sending out packages to galleries and clients.

The remaining five hours, she committed to going to one to three events a week where she would have quality conversations with people, give out her business card and collect business cards, and then add people to her mailing list, ensuring she followed up with them.

We discovered after a few weeks of her being on this schedule that initially she wasted a lot of time. She had to acclimate herself to having a fixed schedule. For someone who has never done this in relation to their creative time, it can be very challenging. She then found, within a few weeks of planning and tracking her time, that she was growing all areas of her business in leaps and bounds.

As someone who has done short-term and long-term planning over many years, I knew this was one of the results she would experience. Once she got some early wins, she became even more excited and streamlined about planning her time and what she could accomplish with it. She cut out extra social media time that was not serving her business growth. She started getting up earlier so she could schedule in exercise that previously she did not have time for. She was doing active sales and marketing work and she really grew!

The reality for some artists is they initially need to spend more time creating a body of work. Often when they come out of graduate school or early on, artists don't have that many paintings available, which makes it challenging for people to become interested in their work. They actually have to spend time creating 10 to 15 works of art which they can then photograph and then market.

Early on, with determining a schedule, an artist might say: "I really need to spend more of that time making my art, so I have something to market and sell to someone."

This is a weekly process. If you do this consistently every week, at the end of the month you might find you've put in 100 quality hours (or more) of studio time, writing time, professional development time, marketing time and networking time. That's when you'll really start to see an artist's career take off in an exciting way, because they're covering everything.

The overall goal is to get to 95% of your time actually making what you want to make and being the creative in the studio. If you put in focused and clear work on your career, you will eventually have galleries. You will have patrons. You will have people that are buying your art based on the foundational work you did initially. At some point, the scales tip and you have people coming to you. Things will get easier. You have your art selling off your website or your galleries are selling it and you have to keep up with the exhibitions and demands. You're not doing very much other than making the art, putting it up, or getting it out to people. That's really the dream.

One of the challenges in building an art career is patience. Most people put in work and energy and want to see results immediately. It can take some time to see a result from your hard work. What I have found over the years is that developing gratitude for what is happening and what you have the ability to do can bring things to you faster! What is an attitude of gratitude? It is being grateful for what you have and what you have the ability to create around you each day. Some of the things you might say to yourself are: I am so grateful that I get to build a career that I love. I am so grateful that I get to share my creativity with the world and that I have been given these gifts. I am grateful for all of the people in my life that show up for me and support me and care about what I am doing. I am grateful that I have the ability to talk with people about my art ideas and what I am most excited about.

When something positive happens for you, such as a sale of your art or services, it is also important to cultivate gratitude for these happenings on a consistent basis, as then more positivity will follow! You might find yourself saying: I am grateful for this sale and money so that I can continue to build my passion and career. I am grateful that someone connected with my work enough to want to include it in their home. I am grateful that I have the ability to inspire others through my art.

Gratitude is a powerful tool and strategy for growing your business. I start each day by writing down 3-10 things I am most grateful for each morning. It can extend to all areas of your life. Try it and watch the goodness snowball!

ACTION STEPS:

- Take a piece of paper and draw three columns. In the first column, write down all of the things you like to do as an artist if money and time were no object.
- In the second column, write down all of the things that you don't like to do.
- In the third column, make a list of the things you don't like to do that you could potentially find someone else to do or things that you don't like doing which you could potentially change your attitude and learn how to love doing.
- The point is, though you do not yet know how it will happen, to identify the things you could potentially outsource or things you could get better at doing.
- An example from my list of things I love to do would be meeting with clients. In my column of things that I don't like to do is bookkeeping, and in the third column of outsourcing I would write "finding a bookkeeper."

- In addition, in my third column early on I had email marketing. I knew I didn't like it because I found it to be daunting. Once I started reading more about it and how to do it effectively, I actually became excited to experiment with it and see what I could create with it. Now it is something that I continue to love to do, although I outsource all of the design and uploading to my assistants! I concentrate on writing the copy and content.

KEY TAKEAWAYS:

- Part of your plan should be to plan.
- Consider outsourcing what you really don't like to do.
- Whatever your plan might be, an even smarter plan exists.
- Develop an attitude of gratitude

Case Study:

The Entrepreneur Who Planned His Way To The Top

Tariq Johnson is an entrepreneur and former Financial Advisor who has managed up to $60 million in client's assets and has also become a juice bar franchise owner with successful locations in California and Florida. In addition, he spent a year speaking to Fortune 500 companies in association with Tony Robbins as a peak performance strategist, doing workshops and giving talks throughout the United States while honing his speaking skills.

For many years, Tariq dreamed of being a successful entrepreneur, but circumstances either prevented or delayed him from doing so. During these years, he kept himself going in his role as a successful financial advisor, finding opportunities for advancement, climbing the corporate ladder, and earning more money. Being a motivational speaker and coming into contact with entrepreneurs and business owners eventually reinvigorated his dream of ownership for which he long had a plan on paper.

Tariq finally decided to just do it, and with his business partner he invested in his first franchise located in California. It took a while to get the location open, during which time Tariq had to utilize his business and financial skillsets first to learn the business and then to train a manager and employees. With his practiced eye for business details and his experience with customer service, as well as with his focus on high operational execution, in a year's time he developed his business into one of the parent company's top franchises. Most new business owners struggle in their first few years to become profitable, but with Tariq's drive, organization, planning and diligence, his first franchise became profitable within two months of opening. Earnings continued to increase each month and year thereafter along with his business performance stats as compiled by the parent company.

His next move was to invest in a second franchise when he and his wife moved to Florida. This second franchise presented Tariq with a unique opportunity because it was located in a smaller community and had been struggling due to a lack of organization and the need for a streamlined operation and better marketing. This second business has now begun to thrive under

Tariq's leadership and will have its most profitable year to date.

What contributed to Tariq's outstanding success from the start? Tariq attributes his success to his ability to be completely clear in his objectives with regard to what he wants to achieve and how he plans to achieve it. His years helping clients develop their financial plans and then utilize these plans to guide their choices and actions gave him his own template to do the same for his businesses. His abilities with financials, planning, budgeting and tracking is another important skillset. He does the financial planning for his businesses and lets the numbers tell him where he is succeeding and where he might need to make an improvement.

Tariq says that: "Without having a really thoughtful, strategic plan, executing that plan, and then adapting, there's no way I would have been as successful as I have been with my businesses."

His top planning tip for entrepreneurs is to: create a crystal-clear vision of what you want to create in your business. For example, if you are a builder who is building a home for a homeowner and executing their vision, you need to know every relevant detail in order to be able to build it exactly as they are imagining it! In creating a vision for what you want to create, write out every detail down to the smallest of details, including how much money you want to make, the amount of gross sales you want, after tax profits, and what you want your business to look like. How you are thinking about your business and your mindset and vision is crucial to creating its success!

Tariq's entrepreneurial path keeps growing and expanding,

and becomes more exciting as he now plans to launch his next (online) business. Tariq has proven the practicality of his ability to combine new visions with his planning skills, and with them he will surely continue to produce more success.

7. Out of the Studio

IDEALLY, MOST CREATIVES should spend 95% of their time doing what they love which is creating. For me as a gallery dealer, curator and coach, I prefer to spend my time in the act of curating, selling art or looking at art and working with artists and clients. The reality is, if I am going to accomplish my goals, it means getting out there in the public in various ways. This is no different for artists, irrespective of your focus and genre.

With our world globally interconnected and our having information at our fingertips on the Internet, it has become easier than ever to connect with people and find information. Besides being known for the work being produced, as a creative it is also important to be known for what you are producing or why you are making your art. This is the next level of recognizing that you want to be a working professional creative. It's not just about the work you're producing, but about the creative behind the work. It's about who you are and what's your why.

It is not enough these days to sit in your studio producing or even sit posting online. I believe you still need to get out there. What's more, there is power in communities and what they can do to support and help each other.

I have a fun story to share that illustrates this, as I have continued to watch this phenomenon grow. In 2016, I did a workshop, around the launch of my first book, for 50 artists on how to build a successful art career, and I had it in my gallery. I advertised it online and through email and only had room to seat 50 people. I didn't know who was going to show up. Although I was happy writing my book, I had to nudge myself to get the book out there and actually market it. As I said, artists need to let people know who they are along with the work they're making. We need to market ourselves.

I knew that during this workshop it was important for me to promote myself as an author and to launch my book, and also to provide value for artists and share with them some of what I talked about in the book. I had more than 50 artists sign up, which I was very happy about. Five of the artists attending were friends of mine whom I urged to come, as I wanted to fill least a few seats. This meant that there would be around 45 artists whom I didn't know.

Most of the attendees came from Philadelphia and elsewhere in Pennsylvania, with a couple coming from New Jersey. One flew in from Georgia and a few drove in from New York. We were all in the room that night for four hours and I really enjoyed doing my first reading and teaching about some of the principles that I thought were important to growing a career. At the end of the evening, I set up a Facebook group so that people in the workshop could connect with each other. This meant I could continue to share with them, and I hoped some of the artists would share their experience trying the content after the workshop. I hoped maybe some of them would set studio dates or at least get together and talk about their work.

Several years later, as a result of one workshop, these artists have shared many stories about meeting that evening for the first time. Some of them have helped each other get into exhibitions or have pitched group exhibitions of their work. A few have purchased each other's works online. I've come to know their artwork through our online interactions, and I've sold some of their artworks through my art advisory firm.

Some of them have started new businesses or expanded existing businesses, some began working with other artists in that group. One attendee who started a magazine has featured some of the artists that were in the workshop that evening in the publication and has made friends and connections. What the story highlights for me is the importance of putting yourself out there, of being in a room with other people. It doesn't matter if it's a gallery exhibition or going to a museum opening. Just by meeting people, shaking hands with people and interacting with the world, you never know what magic will come of it.

I couldn't have imagined that a couple years after this workshop I would have coached some of these artists. I did not envision that I would have placed some of them in art collections and that some of them would have collaborated on exhibitions together. I've had people tell me one of the best things that happened to them in the last couple of years was joining that group, and part of this, besides connecting and opportunities, was realizing for these artists was that they were not alone.

This story was a reminder to me to share with artists the power of community and physically being out in the world, and not just to sit behind a phone or a desk or in your studio, and how this can impact your art work and business for many years to come.

I will say, though, that it takes a proactive approach and, for some artists, getting over their fear of being around people they don't know.

I like watching how artists interact in different situations, and many times when artists do get out, they tend to stand around not talking with anyone or stand in groups with other artists drinking wine. Connecting with the right people and/or meeting new people does not happen if you are not willing to put yourself out there. It is imperative as creatives to go up to someone looking at your work on the wall and introduce yourself or put yourself in shows or situations where you can meet others that can help you further and grow your career and to connect. This means meeting with collectors, curators, artists, consultants and creative people from your community who are going out to events. Everyone is there for a reason. Why not find out and see if you can create a magical situation for yourself? What is there to lose?

It is a great pleasure for me to bring together diverse people from different backgrounds with different aims who end up connecting and who start to co-create together.

As for my workshop example, to me it highlights that people who didn't know each other, who were strangers in the same place at the same time, started collaborating based on the experience of the workshop and the Facebook group. They started saying things like:

"I like your work. Oh, well let's collaborate."

"Oh, I'm doing a call to art, send in your info."

"I like this piece of art. How much is it?"

Events like this have a life of their own in ways that we don't imagine when we set them up. I only hoped that people would connect, because the bottom line for many creatives is that they're alone in the studio. The nature of an artist's work doesn't put them around other people. This means they often miss out on opportunities to collaborate and to have people know who they are.

So, the question to ask yourself is: How can I as a creative consistently interact with the world and meet with people?

Part of it is taking some time out of your schedule and putting yourself out there and using your intuition.

Does an event sound like something that could be interesting or useful for you to go to?

When you ask yourself if this going to be helpful for you, be quiet and see what comes up. If you are just 50% certain that it is going to be helpful for you, follow your intuition, put yourself in some of these places, just relax and see what can come of putting yourself out there a little bit.

I recently did just that, although it was not without a small struggle. I had an event I was supposed to attend in Philadelphia, while I was in my California office. When I knew the date, I put it on my calendar and usually I block out 5-7 days around the event to organize other client meetings, to make the trip more worthwhile. As the event was getting closer, I realized I really had no purpose or reason to be in Philadelphia except this one three-hour event.

My intuition was telling me to book a $700 ticket to go, but my logical mind was talking me out of it saying: "You don't really need to spend that money to go, and you have nothing else going on, so why waste your time."

I could not really justify it, but I decided to listen to my intuition, booked the ticket and went. It ended up being a wonderful event, I connected with a lot of people I had not seen in years and met some interesting new people who had come to see the collection I had curated.

One of those people that evening, who I met for the first time, was sitting on a committee several months later making a decision regarding a project that I was part of. He was the decisive factor in a major proposal and it all came together for me in an instant. Sometimes you don't know why you are being drawn to do something or go somewhere, even when it does not make logical sense to your brain. I realized meeting that person helped me create a new business situation and I was incredibly grateful that I decided to follow my intuition and not my logic! It literally paid off in dividends.

I think a lot of artists end up thinking of these situations as 'competitive' where they are in the company of other creatives. I think a nicer mindset is to actively seek out the possibilities of collaboration and co-creation.

This is especially true for creatives, as their nature is to create! Some of this can be very simple, such as having people to the studio and having people ask you questions about what you're making. Just having the chance to talk about what you're making, outside of actually making it, can open new doors. Wonderful opportunities can come from this; often we forget that creatives are patrons of artists as well. I've had artists tell me that one of their greatest pleasures is having other artists buy their art.

I see a large part of my curator and gallery role as collaborative. I collaborate on design ideas, on commissions and often on the vision of an art collection. I also see the artist and the clients as collaborators.

There are great places to hang out online and to connect. On social media sites like Facebook, you get not a writer's group or an artist's group per se, you get a creativity group. These groups focus on bringing people together and finding out how to be better creators and how to better collaborate. The interesting thing about creating and interacting is you don't necessarily need to leave your house, although I recommend it.

You can collaborate with people online and never have met that person. You can share ideas and someone might see it and interact with it in return and then, all of a sudden, you're in a dialogue with someone around the world, and you just don't know where that will lead. So, there's this really interesting global connectivity happening right now through artists having the chance to very easily share their work on social media and via their websites. Now, they've opened their studio doors to the world and people often will show up from somewhere unexpected wanting to collaborate with that artist, whether it's a commission or a writing project or a dance project. This global reach creates an interesting phenomenon in which people on different parts of the planet are giving each other access to their own local tribes.

I recommend that artists make it a priority to put into their weekly or monthly schedules time when they're going to an event to meet people in person; and that they also actively invite people into their studio or share their work with people in person. If artists can't get out physically, then at least they should be active on social media. There are lots of creative forums that artists can join online to have that connectivity with groups of artists.

Also, there are lots of places where you can put your work up in a way that it can also produce a stream of conversations, if you like. You can use a blog or a podcast. You could use Instagram or YouTube.

For many years musicians and writers have gone digital. Now, too, there are an increasing number of sites that offer virtual galleries and e-commerce for print, canvas and digital downloads for artists.

ACTION STEPS:

- Where could you go locally to meet people or be in places that could be helpful for you professionally? Pick one or two events right now and put them on your calendar.
- Do you use your intuition when deciding what you should do or not do? Test it out next time by asking yourself if something would be helpful or not for you to attend. If the answer is yes, attend the event and see if you can understand why you were being pulled in that direction. Remember the positive situations that come out of these moments and get better at listening to

your intuition.

- ⊚ Are there creative groups you have heard about that you have been meaning to join? Pick one right now and take 5 minutes to join! A year from now, track 3 positives that came out of joining this group. If nothing has come out of it within 3 months, join another.

KEY TAKEAWAYS:

- ⊚ Especially when you start out as an artist, nobody knows you exist.
- ⊚ Fellow artists are potential allies, not competitors.
- ⊚ Expect the unexpected when you venture out of the studio.

Case Study:

The Chief Creative Officer Who, By Getting Out of the Office, Inspires Growth and Creativity

Patrick Hardy is the Chief Creative Officer at Tierney Communications, an industry leading, full-service communications agency headquartered in Philadelphia. He has been with the company for more than 21 years and has consistently advanced in position and accomplishment. The work culture at Tierney Communications thrives on the thinking of its 115 creative minds encompassing multiple disciplines. Throughout his career, Patrick has helped make known such notable brands as Verizon, TD Bank, Independence Blue Cross, Martin Guitar, and Comcast.

Patrick is comfortable wearing the different hats required of him by being a creative himself, while also being a senior executive who leads a team. He is a natural people person and a connector. These qualities inspire his thinking in ways that are different from those creatives who can't get out of the studio or the office.

When he started at Tierney's former Broad Street location, Patrick could often be found, along with many of his colleagues, in the local Rizzoli bookstore looking through art and photography books which were one of his sources of inspiration. He is an avid traveler, people watcher, and art connoisseur; he not only loves looking at fashion, style and "color". He also is very interested in the texture of materials and clothing. He studies fashion more deeply to inspire his work.

For Patrick, inspiration can come from anywhere: literature, taking a walk in the neighborhoods of Philadelphia, an interesting conversation, his "old school" love of magazines, as well as from inside the offices of Tierney.

Tierney recently relocated its headquarters to a newly designed space. It was Patrick who helped lead the executive management team's initiative to select the art, furniture, textures, and design materials, and to design the space so that its ambience would be a daily inspiration to employees. When you enter Tierney's space, you encounter surprising flashes of artistic inspiration and color around the offices. There are giant collaboration screens as well as music—from Reba McEntire to Kanye West, that all the employees curate together. Patrick is cognizant of the need always to remember that people are inspired by different things, whether it's music, art, design, technology, sound or architecture. Tierney wanted to create a beautiful and stimulating environment in which to nourish this aspect in their employees' work and also to inspire their clients who frequent the space.

When, many years ago, Patrick was just completing a graduate advertising program, he noticed there was not much information, apart from the creative work of advertising, about how to build a successful advertising business. He was determined to make it to the top of his profession, and therefore he sought out situations that could put him in contact with the people, learning, and stimulation to catalyze his professional growth.

Although a natural people person, he did not always feel comfortable or unafraid attending networking events by himself. At the time, "personal growth" meant going out to events, meeting with people, and discovering the positive takeaways from the meeting to help one keep learning and making connections. When he was younger, Patrick would set mini-goals for himself, such as going to an event once a week and making connections that would lead to other connections. He learned to enjoy these situations which led him to meet new clients, gain new inspiration and ideas, and to be stimulated by his work.

One of these events was the C2-MTL conference which takes place each year in Montreal and is hosted by Sid Lee, Fast Company and Cirque du Soleil. Patrick "forced" himself to go the first year, as it was not in his nature to attend large, several-day events by himself. He spent those days with a few hundred creatives in collaborative, odd, and sometimes uncomfortable situations (like brainstorming blindfolded in a ball pit and sitting in chairs suspended up in the air with just a net underneath).

From this initial experience came twenty pages of notes which inspired him to think differently about the communications business and about how to make more connections within the departments of Tierney. As a result, the company experienced a large growth phrase, which literally was inspired by their "getting out of the office", out of their comfort zone, and letting go of the idea "this is how we've always done it".

Patrick relates: "It was not meeting one particular person or a new client *per se*, but the opportunity to immerse myself in collaborative and unusual situations that spurred notes upon notes of ideas on how to grow the business. It was such a successful experience for me that I went back two additional years."

These days, you will find Patrick as a member of several boards; he is also involved with the Philadelphia Museum of Art's marketing committee. He also donates his time and skills to the Association for Public Art and to Philadelphia's premier contemporary dance company, BalletX. He is inspired by what he contributes as well as by learning from other people around him, whether it be an accountant, an artist, or a performer. Patrick loves being an active, engaged contributor to the art and cultural life of the City of Philadelphia.

Tierney recently received an award from the Americans for the Arts for its Business Committee for the Arts program, which recognized the company for its exceptional involvement with the Arts. Patrick says that Tierney has a year-round focus on being involved in the Arts in Philadelphia in ways that enrich their workplace, education opportunities, and the community. The entire Tierney management team strongly believes that the Arts guide one of their core tenets: 'Inspire Curiosity'.

It is abundantly evident that Patrick's curiosity continues to evolve. He continues to find fun, connective and innovative ways through which to bring what inspires him, when he gets out of the office, back to his work environment, which in turn help one of the Northeast's leading communications companies to grow.

8. Finding the Helpers

IF YOU HAVE gotten yourself out of the studio, well done!

You're out there in the world, touting your work and having some degree of success. You're making inroads, finding people that like your art; people are buying your art and the people that are buying your art are maybe telling other people. But how do you amplify these initial successes? How do you find people that can really help you go stratospheric?

Many artists and creatives might not initially realize that finding helpers is an integral part of building their career. Initially a helper could be an adviser in graduate school. Helpers could be families, parents or friends that might actually be your first collectors or financial supporters. Later in your career helpers could be art consultants or advisors, mentors and gallery owners, agents and coaches.

Depending on what your craft is, and what your creative work is, whether you're a writer, a dancer, a playwright, a graphic designer, an artist or a musician, it pays dividends to discover who in the community can help elevate you, support you and also help you connect with other people in your respective industry.

It will be only slightly different for each creative endeavor.

Part of your process should be to study other successful people and learn how they were able to build a career by finding people around them to help elevate them. When I started my business in 2001, the first round of my helpers were artists. Without these people, when I did not have artists to exhibit, I wouldn't really have had a business. The first stage in my finding these helpers was curating the best artists for my program at the time.

Pretty quickly on, I realized that for me to stay in business, I needed to find the next tier of helpers, who would actually purchase art, write about the art I was showing, and publicize my business for me. So, I moved into phase two, in which I identified art collectors, arts writers and people that would publicize my gallery and exhibitions. Part of this was having openings, doing mailings and developing a mailing list. As I've continued, the types of helpers have grown exponentially; there's typically a snowball effect when people start hearing about what you're doing creatively. Friends will tell other friends.

We all have to start somewhere. In 2001, I literally had zero clients. My first client was a taxicab driver. My next client was a corporate client. My next client was the mother of one of the artists I was exhibiting. She then told her best friend about the gallery and her purchase. She became a helper and a buyer, and very quickly it kept snowballing. One sale led to the next and the next and people were talking, and writers were reviewing the exhibition, and it kept going on. That's one way to find the helpers.

In the literary world, a writer can get a literary agent. For the modern artist, the equivalent would be a gallerist, an art manager or a coach. For a dancer, it might be working with a known choreographer and a known studio. In addition, the places where business is being transacted, they're the actual supporters; they can help promote and get the creative person's name and work out there.

Someone asked me recently if there is such a lovely, magical person, who is a very wealthy patron and philanthropist, who loves an artist's work, and maybe buys the work, and then tells all their very rich friends about it.

I would say yes, as I have met such people on a number of occasions. I have collectors who have the money to purchase art, who love my vision and my program, and who trust me as they add to their collections. Often, they fall in love with and obsessively collect particular artists' works over many years. When you establish your name in the community, and then nationally, that in itself will help you attract various types of patrons.

In addition, with technology and many people having access to content through the Internet and social media, people are joining fundraising websites or putting projects on these sites to connect with people who are interested in helping to fund such projects and artists' dream projects.

One year, I was funding residencies for artists to travel to research particular topics and be inspired, and I mentioned it to a client who asked a question about a particular artist. I let him know about the residency and why it was important and he ended up contributing $2500 toward expenses. Another client, who ran out of wall space and who could no longer purchase art, ended up contributing to a book project for another artist, because she wanted to stay engaged with the artist and the gallery.

I recently worked with an artist, who received a grant through a foundation that a patron of the Arts had funded, for her to do a residency. The patron wanted to know what artist the foundation had selected for the grant. When she learned the answer, she found the artist and purchased some of the artist's paintings. All of these scenarios happened because myself and the artists were proactive in sharing their aims and ambitions.

None of this, of course, is anything new. If you're a student of Art History, you're undoubtedly familiar with the Renaissance Period. Patronage, especially in support of the churches, was how work got completed. People gave money to artists like Michelangelo to paint his murals, and this practice of patronage continues today. I don't know if it's talked about as much, but I know from my business, over many years, I've had patrons who have been incredibly supportive of a particular artist, or a particular program. I might have had someone, over the years, who has collected and spent several hundred thousand dollars in being a patron to my business and my vision.

These magical people are out there, and some of them just want to help. They want you to ask them for their help or their support, and that's something I've learned a lot about over the years. I didn't realize early on that part of finding a helper is actually putting yourself out there and simply asking. Many people will see that as a weakness, but it's actually a strength. Not only do you get to connect with someone on a deeper level and share your business or idea or what you are going through, you give people the opportunity to add their own value to your life and work; and if they can't, they can usually help you find someone who can.

I was recently approached by a curator asking me to recommend an artist for a prominent mural project in Philadelphia. I pitched an artist to her who I felt would be worthy of the project and represent the city of Philadelphia, and for whom the project was worthy of her career level. After several rounds of pitching this artist, the artist had an opportunity to make her own presentations, which resulted in her being selected. The curator thanked me, as did the artist; it was a win-win on many levels. All of this came from someone asking me to help them make a recommendation and then wanting to be pitched on the why.

Finding your helpers also creates a cycle of giving, receiving and adding value in an industry. Initially, I didn't want to burden other people, and there was a time when I felt very vulnerable and I didn't actually want to admit that I needed help. I've realized there are a lot of people who get a positive and uplifting feeling from supporting those around them, and in particular business owners. Especially when I was a younger, struggling art dealer, I probably could have gotten more help if I had just simply asked for it.

One friend told me about how he wrote books on mindfulness, and how to de-stress, and he offered them to a dentist for his waiting room. The dentist told him a year later that they were the best thing for his patients, because they got into the dentist chair feeling relaxed. He loved that the books were in the reception area! He helped the dentist and the dentist helped him get more readers.

Artists, and especially those starting out, can put their art in a coffee shop, or a public space, and the business owner becomes a helper by allowing their customers to see something new with which they are not familiar! I have sold many a work of art by having it hung in unlikely places outside of a gallery!

Helpers are everywhere. You are surrounded by them. The challenge for most creatives is to give the necessary time to thinking about where they might be. When you go out into the world, just imagine everyone you meet is a potential helper. Whether it's a dentist office or a coffee shop, or someone in a museum, or a neighbor, or a business owner that supports various projects, or even an individual who might help with grant money.

I was recently walking down a sidewalk in Philadelphia looking at all the buildings and people walking by and started to wonder where I might find my next potential helpers. I smiled as I said to myself: "I don't know him, I don't know her. I haven't been in that building yet or that building."

Another important element, especially if you are a painter or visual artist, but it equally applies to any creative, is to have a business card with your website address and maybe an image on it. Carry a postcard of your artwork or examples on your phone that you can share with people. You might have a sample of music, or a sample of writing, just something that when you're out and at an event or in a moment and someone asks you about your work that you can share. If you could play a short musical sample, or let them read something you've written, or share something visually, or even share a short video, that can immediately connect people with what you're doing.

That's the cool thing with technology. It's created this immediacy of people connecting and sharing. I save a lot of images and stuff on my phone, so I have a whole folder, and I can pull that up if I want to share something with someone. If I also happen to be out of business cards, which happens to me often, as I give them out a lot, I make a point to put the person's name, number and email in my phone and follow-up with them by sending them information.

A writer friend asked me if there is a subtle aspect to finding helpers that's important here. In thinking about the stages of my business, I would say there is. There was a time when I was slightly desperate for money and new clients. I was also a little over eager and probably turned off some of those potential helpers. Then, as I became more relaxed and comfortable in my business, in my vision and what I was up to, I found myself attracting more helpers by letting them find me. I was ready and aware for when they came along, and sometimes they would show up in the strangest guises, like that taxi cab driver who was an art collector!

To let helpers find you, you have to be in a space of openness and receptivity, which encourages a flow of things coming to you. You are in a space of thinking about what you want–goals, visions, dreams and outcomes, instead of the opposite, which is the state of a very desperate, overly-eager person who is forcing something and almost blocking things coming to them. I've noticed that when artists are relaxed, and in their zone, and in more of a joyous state of doing what they love doing, more things happen for them. Note that staying inside your studio is not a receptive state; it's hiding from the helpers.

I have personally found that when I'm not even asking or looking, sometimes that's when the most happens for me. It is then that the people show up who want to help with what I'm doing or even want to use me to help them with something. What goes around comes around. Those who have been helped up the ladder in the past often become the best helpers.

With other artists whom you notice in other media, there is also a great opportunity to combine helpers whereby you could take their artistic output and your artistic output, take one and one and make three. One classic example of this is an artist designing the front cover of a record or a CD or illustrating a book. The collaborative process, when creatives come together, can be incredibly powerful and fun. Collaboration can help elevate everyone involved and promote the project to another level. The ability to learn and work together with other creatives really can advance your own career by leaps and bounds.

In some cases, artists and creatives worry about collaboration because they don't want to surrender control of their projects. They may fear that the person working with them, or from whom they're seeking assistance, might take over the entire project. I would recommend to just give it a shot, with the attitude that you have nothing to lose; see what comes of the collaboration, to learn if you should continue it in the future. Some of the best projects I have worked on were because the clients or the artists contributed an idea or a suggestion that elevated the project.

Also, the other benefit is that you share the marketing effort when you work with someone else. You might be sharing the revenues between two or more people, but it's a real help having someone else to help keep you focused, to give you deadlines and a new level of motivation, commitment and accountability.

ACTION STEPS:

- Ask yourself who, so far in your career, have your helpers been? Make a list and identify who they are, to get your mind warmed up to thinking about them.
- Have your helpers been your parents, employers, teachers, employers in college or even authors who wrote books that inspired you? To know where you want and need to go, it is important to know where you have come from and who has already helped you along the way!
- Make a list of the top 2-5 people around you whom you have wanted to ask for help, and ask two of them now, or two people who know them, for help.
- Ask yourself if there are other creatives or artists in your industry who you know who could be possible helpers. Some of the most obvious people are right in front of us. Make a list of a few people and take the first step of asking one or more of them for help!

KEY TAKEAWAYS:

- Asking for help is not a weakness.
- Helpers often come in strange guises, at strange times.
- Helpers like to help and like to be asked.
- Sometimes they will help you in ways that you didn't know you needed help with.

Case Study:

Author & Marketing Guru Serving People

Seth Godin is an author, speaker, and leader. He has written nineteen best-selling books. Having launched and sold multiple businesses, his influence extends far and wide within business circles. His books are usually read by business executives and not necessarily creatives; their content, though, is wholly applicable to artists, as for example in his recent book titled *This is Marketing: You Can't Be Seen Until You Learn to See* (Portfolio 2018).

I interviewed Seth about how creatives can find their career helpers or their tribe. His book *Tribes* (Penguin 2008) does a deep dive on this topic, and includes topics such as what a tribe is and leadership concepts related to tribes. From the outside looking in, it seemed to me that throughout his career, Seth has created multiple successful tribes. However, I quickly learned that he does not believe it likely that someone will have a tribe and that he claims he does not have a tribe! He explained that a tribe is a "group of people that would be there whether or not you existed." And he further explained: "If one is able to set their ego aside they will understand that a tribe is not yours *per se*; you are there to serve a tribe and they are not there to serve you."

We went on to discuss how in 1995 Fast Company magazine was started in answer to the needs of a group of about a million entrepreneurs and forward thinkers who were disconnected, who wanted to be connected, and who were hungry to make something better but didn't know that others like them even existed. Fast Company was essentially creating a tribe and bringing people together in service to the greater good of the group. The magazine was a major turning point in our culture because it let people find other like-minded people who could connect and be inspired by and learn from one another. Seth happened to be Fast Company's most prolific writer and this made him a narrative guide for these people and helped him find ideas, people and situations, and in turn be found.

During the same period, he was also developing multiple projects, companies and ideas for the Internet, which was a different tribe. At that time, Internet users were largely a group of geeks and nerds using a certain kind of technology for a certain purpose. Seth provided a narrative for them and helped create permission marketing (which is basically every email that you have ever received that you wanted to receive).

After selling his company and leaving Yahoo, he began to write books that address where artists, spiritual leaders, and technology people intersect. Folks who want to make the world better all coming together, their tribes bumping into each other, and Seth narrating for them what might be possible. He is currently running workshops, seminars and an online school called altMBA which has 3,000 graduates from 74 countries. They can connect and meet each other on their own as if they are long lost family members. These people are a tribe but they are not Seth's tribe.

Being of service within a community and serving people is something Seth has done in his own distinctive ways through all of his businesses and books since the 1970s.

From our discussion about creatives, the arts, and the challenges people in the arts face (including fear), here are some key takeaways:

What is available to creatives is a chance to realize that there are a few people, not very many, who want you to succeed and you can serve them. (Seth pointed out that Andy Warhol's career was 'made' by the support of 50 people, which is 48 more than many creatives have).

You only need a few people supporting you to do work that matters (many fewer than what many creatives think they need).

Artists need to stop waiting for people to come and to see who shows up. They need to notice people and go serve them, find the group they want to serve and do it.

Most struggling artists are not really making work that deserves true fans.

You can't get over fear of failure and criticism. You cannot make important art without fear. It won't go away if you are making important art, but you can figure out where to put it so you can carry on and continue despite it.

Most people these days don't read books and don't continue to learn. If you are going to hire yourself and not pay experts to help you to do some of the things you need to do to build a successful career (such as marketing and finance), then don't be an amateur about it. Go learn it!

9. The Modern Artist's Way

ASK YOURSELF, AS if looking back 100 years from now, what's the landscape like for artists, writers, dancers, photographers, playwrights, art directors right now? Do you want to be recognized while you are living or after you're gone?

It is interesting to think about all creatives going through challenges we have experienced such as recessions and where we are now in the modern world within all our creative industries including art, graphic design, dance, music, you name it. Even in my current stage of business, in which I have over 20 years' experience creating my own business as well as working with other creatives I have seen so much happen. I have worked through several recessions and also changes within technology. I've seen a lot of progress happen for people due to their increased accessibility to information which has helped them with their creative process and the realization of their ideas and dreams.

Nowadays, we have both an increased sense of community and commonality as well as access to a huge community of helpers. We are now able to market and advertise our work, not just in our home town, as formerly we only could do through local town newspapers, churches, neighbors or word of mouth. We can expand our marketing reach across the globe. We are living in the most globally interconnected time that we've ever witnessed.

So, as a creative, you have amazing opportunities nowadays to make an impact and a difference in the world, such that you can truly be the change you want to be. A meditation teacher mentioned to me that he noticed, when his meditations have gone live on an app, and when he wakes up in the morning in the UK, Australia's been meditating, then Asia's been meditating, then Europe starts meditating, then it moves over to the United States, first to the East Coast, then to the West coast, then Hawaii. So, literally, the whole world can wake up to your art, which is incredible.

There is another opportunity, especially for Millennials for whom maybe cash is a bit tight and who are not even thinking about pensions. By creating a portfolio of art, you're also creating what could also be a financial portfolio for the future.

Anything you're creating—whether it's dance moves, writings, songs, painting or sculpting, that's your portfolio and your intellectual property. You can get a real financial return on the investment of time you spend creating it. Nowadays, there are wonderful opportunities to produce an outstanding portfolio and share it widely.

For those who are of an older generation and might think that they don't know how to do this, or have time to do it, or how to even start, there are a lot of free website resources available. There's even very cheap labor to help creatives get their portfolio, their websites and their videos put together. You can help others help you.

For those artists who find marketing a bit tedious, one way around it is to be creative about your marketing. Think how examples of your art can advertise your portfolios. People love humor and will share things they find funny. Can you create cartoons that make people smile or do a double take? More simply, let people see an artist at work.

If you want to take a more prescriptive approach, I would also suggest reading as much as you can. I learned a lot in my early days about marketing through reading many books on the subject. I have read books on creating websites, on building an email list, on doing proper email marketing, and on writing marketing letters and doing mailings. I learned much and was able to implement what I learned, to see the results, whether positive or negative, and then make further changes.

Some artists complain that with the Internet everything is free. They post images and content and do not make any money from it. I agree, and my personal take is that the Internet is a connecting tool, a learning tool, and a tool to advertise. We are able to quickly get stuff out there to a global audience and also create a new audience.

I recently spoke with an artist who was trying to get more artists, creatives and people to connect with her work, so she decided to do a live video and offer a free painting to folks who put their name in for a random draw. She had hundreds of people emailing her and writing in to put their name in a draw to win a free painting! The lucky painting went to a new patron in Boston. It was a win-win for everyone involved and I thought a great way direct people to her website and find her work.

There are also people out there who are using social media, especially Instagram, to find, what are called, "influencers" in order to connect with them. If you buy their product or support their product, they will in turn promote and sell, or just promote, your product online. That's a really cool exchange of two people sharing and helping each other through marketing. Influencers are Helpers in the guise of a Marketer.

My personal experience is that through advertising online some of what I'm doing, people who have thought about doing something similar will often get in touch with me to learn more. Sometimes I'll get new clients from promoting what I'm currently doing online.

The truth is there's only one thing you can take with you and that's your evolution; and there's only one thing you can leave behind and that's your art. Because of this, I love talking with creatives about their legacy and what it will be. It is something most people, even in their daily lives, aren't really thinking about, because most folks are in survival mode.

Most creatives don't really start thinking about legacy until they're at the end of their careers, because they're so busy on the front end of their career trying to make it and be able to stay in the marketplace.

Here's some closing questions to ask yourself:

Why are you doing what you're doing and who is it for?

What mark are you going to leave in the world?

What are you leaving behind?

Whether it's for your family, your community, the creative world that you're living in, how are you shaping and influencing the world, and what will your legacy be?

These are all very cool and timely questions because by asking them you will give yourself ideas about the direction in which you might be aiming right now.

ACTION STEPS:

- Find a top artist or creative you admire and study their website or marketing and some of the things they have accomplished. Pick an item you believe you could mirror and go after it!
- Pick a marketing topic such as getting more followers on social media and read two articles about it. Take one idea and try it a few times and see what happens.
- Write down 5 ways you would like to leave a legacy with your creative career and in general. Are your actions aligned towards this? What can you do today to get into alignment with your legacy? Take the first step.

KEY TAKEAWAYS:

- Your art is your legacy and might well be your pension.
- There is more opportunity than ever right now for artists.
- Each one of us can be the change we want to be.
- Make people laugh and they will make you smile.

Case Study:

Bridgette Mayer: Grow Up and Create Your Own Art World

In 1996, I was standing in a prestigious gallery holding up a painting with a gallery installer and listening to a client hem and haw. Was the painting going to go up in value in five years and could she flip it? The blue color on the right side did not work with her couch color: maybe she could have her designer recover the couch or would the artist work with a color swatch and shift the color for her? Was she able to get a discount, since her designer recommended she come in? I stood there, a young, just out-of-college art major, wondering how the artist would feel hearing this discussion. I was feeling frustrated; this was not what I imagined art collecting to be. This was not the important work I had imagined doing while working in a gallery. However, I was also a little green, idealistic and naïve about what the 'real' art world was outside of the walls of a studio and a university.

I had spent years devouring art history, artist biographies and life stories, meeting with artists in studios, doing crits of my work and other artists' works and, yes, working in museums, galleries and institutions to develop my resumé to the point where I could land a commercial gallery job.

As various negative experiences accumulated for me in NY, I felt I had made a mistake by going into the art business. With a growing exasperation, and as my paychecks barely paid for my meager living expenses, I started to wonder if my parents were correct when they warned me that I might end up as a starving artist or arts professional.

Through a series of situations that the universe set in motion and well-orchestrated for me, I ended up finding my way to urban, gritty and blue-collar Philadelphia; there I found my home. Brushing aside New York, San Francisco, and my experiences in Taiwan, I set out to understand the art market and community in Philadelphia, and to my delight found that there was room for me. There was space for the work and career I wanted. There was opportunity to create and grow and become.

After five years of real art world experience and perspective, and the distance it gave me from early experiences, I had a realization that changed my thinking and career, and that re-ignited my passion and desire to continue to be in the gallery world.

I realized:

I could create my own Art World: the world I wanted to be in and be a part of; the artists I wanted to work with and foster and be around, the clients I wanted to work with and not the ones I didn't want to work with. I could be the creator of the destiny I wanted to manifest.

I could eschew the New York model or the gallery model, or like with an à la carte menu, I could pick and choose what worked for me and ignore or skip what didn't work for me.

The truth is that all creatives have this opportunity, whether they realize it or not. Ask yourself: What is your journey or destination as a creative?

What I have learned from curating hundreds of shows, by working with thousands of artists and hundreds of clients, is that you, the artist, are in charge. It is your show, your life, your voice. We are all unique and it is each person's unique voice that creates the authenticity that drives a creative career.

Ask yourself: What are you going to do with the time you have on this planet and what will your legacy be?

From the stories I have shared in this book and from the successful people with whom I have interacted with over the years, a few things are clear:

1. Work hard
2. Show up...repeatedly
3. Take chances and keep moving forward
4. Don't listen to people who tell you it will be too hard, or you might starve or fail
5. Create good work that you are proud of, and if you are not proud of something don't waste people's time or put the work out there
6. Keep going, enjoy the journey along the way and not just the destination when you reach it.

This Modern Artist's Way is really up to you. You are a unique individual and artist with your own ideas and voice to offer to the world. Go do it—and don't look back.

Love to all the readers who made it this far and love to all the amazing creative people with whom I have had the pleasure and privilege to work and who continue to teach and inspire me!

Afterword

I WANTED TO write this book to share my business and spiritual insights for a long time. I finally made the move to start writing it when I found out I was pregnant in the fall of 2018. I gave myself a deadline of sending the finished manuscript to the publisher in March, a few weeks before my April due date. I am a planner and work well with deadlines and milestones; I knew it would be challenging to complete the book during a pregnancy, but I wanted to make it happen.

Everything was on track and moving ahead as planned – or so I thought. The one thing I hadn't envisioned was my baby deciding to arrive three weeks early! I was in total disbelief (and then had to smile) when I went for a routine checkup and the doctor told me that they needed to induce labor as soon as possible. They could not tell if the umbilical cord was partially wrapped around the baby's neck and were concerned about a deceleration that showed in the heartbeat.

The "planner" in me went to my mental checklist and realized how many things I'd wanted to finish in the few weeks before baby Caleb arrived – the big one being the manuscript, which was in the last stages of being written. Here I was learning my first lesson as a soon-to-be new mom that time and life would never be the same. My baby was arriving in the same fashion that I had come into the world when I was born, which was quickly and on my own terms.

My priority in that moment was to keep myself and my baby healthy, to let the universe be my guide, and to let go. In the next twenty hours I would keep learning that lesson of letting go.

Nothing about my labor, which included being induced and ultimately having a C-section, went according to plan. I had to let Caleb come into the world on his own terms. Even though I had visualized and planned for the birthing experience I wanted, there is always a greater plan in place – although we don't always know why!

Caleb was born on March 24, 2019 at 7:33pm, weighing a healthy 7lbs. It was a miraculous experience for me, one that was three years in the making with my journey to get pregnant.

I will never forget the first moment I heard Caleb's voice when he cried out and saw his eyes and face as he was placed on my chest on top of my heart. As the tears poured from my eyes, I finally felt complete. Tariq and I snuggled and held him and a little voice in my head sang, "And baby makes three." We had the family we had dreamed of.

As I look back on my recent journey and finally prepare to publish this book, what occurs to me is that the most important things in life are not easy. For me to get pregnant and start a family was not easy. For me to give birth was not easy. For me to write this book and finish it was not easy. Right now, being a mom is not easy. The lessons in this book, and the things I have learned, were not easily won or accomplished. They were not easy.

Often, to triumph in life we have to put in our best and clearest effort, let go a little bit after working hard, trust how things will happen, and what will show up. I hope, dear reader, that sharing this journey with you will help to illuminate more of your path in the world as you build your career as a creative!

Acknowledgments

I would like to thank all the artists I have had the privilege to work with through my gallery and consulting business since 2001. Serving you and your dreams has been one of the things I am grateful for daily and that gives me great joy in my work.

I would like to thank all my clients and patrons who have journeyed with me in many forms since 2001. It has been an honor and a pleasure to do the work I get to do with you and for you to enliven your world through art!

I would like to thank my mom and dad and extended family for your love and belief in me and for your curiosity and enjoyment in hearing my stories!

I would like to thank everyone who was involved in getting this book together from concept outlining to printing and all of the immense details. Your hard work and creativity kept me going!

And lastly and most importantly, I would like to thank my amazing husband Tariq and my adorable baby boy Caleb who I am grateful to be able to call "my family." Tariq, your belief in me and urging me forward helps in more ways than you know. I am excited for all our adventures that are ahead!

About the Author

Bridgette Mayer is an accomplished art dealer, art consultant, author, speaker, coach and mom. Bridgette Mayer Gallery is a private gallery based in Philadelphia representing artists from around the world. Bridgette Mayer Art Advisors deals in secondary market artwork, provides consulting services for individuals, corporations and cities and curates exhibitions and projects in the US.

Bridgette turned to art as a means of escape during a childhood filled with turmoil, and now helps other creatives find their own career success by speaking and coaching creatives globally. Her first book, "The Art Cure" is available on amazon.com.

She currently lives in Orlando, Florida with her husband Tariq and son Caleb and their dogs Buddy and Luca. Bridgette's businesses can be found at:

www.bridgettemayer.com
www.bridgettemayergallery.com
www.bridgettemayerartadvisors.com

CPSIA information can be obtained
at www.ICGtesting.com
Printed in the USA
LVHW082345140120
643674LV00018B/765

9 780578 606927